Management Today mag...
where he was the management columnist betwe...
and 2010. He continues to write for the *FT*, the *Guardia...
and other publications. He is Visiting Professor in management practice at Cass Business School, City, University of London. He was also until recently director of the High Pay Centre, a think tank that looks at the issue of top pay.

how to: ACADEMY launched in September 2013. Since then it has organized over 1000 talks and seminars on Business, Lifestyle, and Science & Technology, which have been attended by 100,000 people. The aim of the series is to anticipate the needs of the reader by providing clarity, precision and know-how in an increasingly complex world.

STEFAN STERN

HOW TO: BE A BETTER LEADER

bluebird
books for life

First published 2019 by Bluebird
an imprint of Pan Macmillan
20 New Wharf Road, London N1 9RR
Associated companies throughout the world
www.panmacmillan.com

ISBN 978-1-5098-2126-6

9 8 7 6 5 4 3 2 1

A CIP catalogue record for this book is available from the British Library.

Typeset in 10.5/14 pt Charter ITC Std by Jouve (UK), Milton Keynes
Printed and bound by CPI Group (UK) Ltd, Croydon, CR0 4YY

Visit **www.panmacmillan.com** to read more about all our books
and to buy them. You will also find features, author interviews and
news of any author events, and you can sign up for e-newsletters
so that you're always first to hear about our new releases.

For my father,
Jan Stern – a quiet leader.

Contents

INTRODUCTION

'What are you in it for?'
– Jim Collins, author of *Good to Great*[1]

The leadership industry is vast, and yet leadership is in crisis. We have rarely talked more about leadership than we do today. But the gap between what we want from our leaders and what we get is huge. We dream and reminisce about John F Kennedy or Franklin D Roosevelt or Winston Churchill. But we look around the world and see an array of demagogues besmirching their offices, or self-serving chief executives being grossly overpaid, dragging the idea and practice of leadership down into the gutter.

This is another – short – book about leadership. Why do we need one, and why have you bought it (or picked it up to look at)? We know that businesses and organizations expect people at all levels to show initiative and display leadership. Perhaps you are a boss, or an aspiring leader, and are looking for a little boost or a few useful ideas.

This book is designed to help. In just a few pages we will consider what it means to be a leader, what good and bad leadership look like, think about a few prominent exceptional leaders, ask about the different ways in which men and women lead (and how we can get nearer to genuine equality at work), examine the language of leaders, and end with a few closing thoughts and prompts to action.

But before going any further: what is the nature of the leadership challenge today? Why do we have a problem with our leaders? And what can we do about it?

The Conservative MP (and former Royal Artillery captain) Johnny Mercer has written candidly about his frustrations with today's leaders. Our problems, he has said,

> . . . require a higher standard of political debate, and a higher standard from our politicians. And that is the most galling thing about the present domestic and international agenda. At a time of profound challenges, we are perhaps enduring one of the most sub-optimal generations of political leaders the world has known. We are fixated by polling, social media reactions, focus groups and think tanks: the days of the visionary, bold, courageous leader seem to be on the wane. [2]

In business, too, the story is not good. There is, as many surveys have shown, a crisis of trust in leaders and how businesses operate. But this supposed crisis of trust, says Robert Phillips, the founder of the Jericho Partners consultancy, is really a crisis of leadership. Elite CEOs do not like to talk about this: 'Locked in echo chambers and wrapped-up in their own machismo, with few notable exceptions, they lack fundamental self-awareness and honesty. They have raised the banality of trust to an art form.'[3]

The writer Margaret Heffernan agrees. 'The crisis of leadership is partly due to the fact that we mostly observe leaders as out for themselves rather than working on our behalf,' she says.[4] These leaders, Heffernan suggests, fail the test set by Jim Collins with his stark question: what are you in it for?

The arts world has noticed this crisis of leadership too.

The musician and lyricist Tim Minchin despairs at what he is seeing.

> Give me a leader who will stand up and talk to us like we're f***ing adults and inspire us to be the best version of ourselves, you know. Where are they? Where's the oratory? Where's the f***ing rhetoric? . . . Obama wasn't perfect but my God that dude could talk . . You don't have to talk dumb – you have to talk clear . . . You don't have to be a f***ing demagogue and rile up the less educated, the less rich, the insecure to turn on themselves . . . I know I don't understand the subtleties of politics – obviously – but just get a f***ing leader who can say the right shit . . . Someone with a good heart, good intentions. Someone who can talk.[5]

If only it were that easy. Leadership is about more than plausible talk, of course (although it helps). Good leaders need self-knowledge. They need to understand their strengths and weaknesses, where their motivation comes from and why they are doing the job they do. Not enough leaders do this essential homework on themselves.

Neil Morrison, HR director at the FTSE100 firm Severn Trent Water, says that knowing about your limitations can help you to be a better leader.

> Truly great leaders recognize they're not as great as others believe and they know how to compensate for it. They're acutely aware of their strengths and weakness, they recognize how they're behaving and why – the situations that will trigger them or cause them to react. And they work constantly to maintain that level of aware-ness . . . If you're on a leadership journey, my advice to

you is to spend a little more time focusing on yourself. Be hard on 'you' in order to give yourself a break. There is no model of leadership perfection that you will ever obtain, but you can be the best leader you're capable of being. There is a path for you to grow and be better, but only you will ever, truly know how.[6]

So far these are familiar, even conventional, concerns. But of course the other fundamental reason why leadership is in crisis is that authority itself is being questioned and traditional hierarchies challenged. The nature of power and how it is wielded is changing. In recent times, dynamic networks and movements have grown up without obvious or conventional leadership structures.

David Brooks in the *New York Times* described these changes well. 'If power in the Greatest Generation [post Second World War] looked like Organization Men running big institutions, and power for the [baby-]boomers looked like mass movements organized by charismatic leaders like Steve Jobs and Barack Obama, power these days looks like decentralized networks in which everyone is a leader and there's no dominating idol,' he wrote.[7]

Some have tried to meet concerns about old-fashioned, top-down leadership with alternative concepts and approaches. 'Distributed' or 'collaborative leadership' implies that not all wisdom is to be found at the top. 'Servant leadership' requires leaders to be humble, and to recognize that they are there to serve others. ('Serve to Lead' is in fact the motto of the British Army's leadership training academy, Sandhurst.) How many CEOs actually got to the top by being more humble than their colleagues remains an open question, however.

These changing times call for what the business leader

Rajeev Peshawaria calls 'open source leadership', where leaders establish a purpose or goal for an organization but then are relaxed and open about where ideas come from.

> I think today we have to open it up to everybody to say, 'Who has a good idea? Who wants to contribute in what way? Submit your projects'. Then make it no barrier to entry and see where the innovation comes from. The people that raise their hands every year and come up with great ideas and are able to back it up with their energy, they're your future leaders. Your innovation takes places in an organic way, and future leadership development takes place in an organic way. The cream rises to the top naturally . . . I think the big change is going to be for leaders to understand what it means to live in the open-source era.[8]

Leadership, like management, is prone to fads and fashions. But while some things change, some stay the same. The task of this book is to avoid falling into the fad trap, and to offer a few useful and, with any luck, timeless observations about how you can be a better leader.

So let's get on with it.

1:

WHAT DOES IT MEAN TO LEAD?

Describe the task in hand ('the vision thing')

Leaders are sense-makers; at least, they ought to be. They define terms. They set targets and establish parameters. They describe the context in which work has to be done. They point the way ahead. Want to be a leader? Then have some sense of where you are and where you want to go. If you don't know, then how is anyone supposed to follow you?

It is a paradox of leadership that, while many may aspire to get to the top, if and when lucky executives get there they may forget that others are now looking to the new leader for that sense of direction, just as they used to before getting the top job. You used to be a face in the crowd. But now the crowd is looking at you. Leaders, in short, are watched and studied much more than many of them perhaps realize.

This is why that skill of describing (or 'framing') the situation is so important. There needs to be a shared understanding throughout the organization of what is required, and what sort of contribution people ought to make. Does this mean that leaders have to be great storytellers? Many will tell you that this is so. There has to be a leadership narrative, it is often said.

The management guru Steve Denning published a fable about leadership and storytelling in 2004, called *Squirrel Inc*, set in a business world inhabited by, yes, squirrels. If you can get over the potentially comic nature of the setting there is a serious message to be grasped about the role of story-telling in leadership. One squirrel explains,

> When you tell a story, you engage us in your experi-ence. You entice us into your life. If we accept the invitation we can get beyond mere facts or chatter. No matter what the story's about we learn who you are. We begin to see things from your perspective. We begin to live your story. With luck, we begin to trust you. Your story becomes my story becomes our story. That's what we need from the CEO. We need to learn who on earth he really is. [9]

This is persuasive. We are often told that the era of 'com-mand and control' leadership is over, which is probably a pretty big overstatement, especially when you think of the conditions so many people in the service and retail sectors have to work in.

But in the higher skilled parts of the 'knowledge econ-omy', where ideas and intangible assets are key, leaders cannot usually just arbitrarily call the shots and tell people what to do. There has to be encouragement, suggestion, persuasion, 'nudging' rather than shoving. We will listen to leaders we believe in. But we cannot believe in leaders whom we do not know, who are physically and emotionally remote and rarely present. We will listen to good storytellers we feel close to and like the look of.

The vision thing

The first President Bush, George H (the forty-first US President), was preparing to run for the White House in 1987 to succeed Ronald Reagan in the 1988 election. It was suggested he needed to take a few days out of Washington, perhaps at Camp David, to develop the big ideas he might base his campaign on. But Bush was not convinced. He dismissed such talk as a waste of time, aimless worrying about 'the vision thing'.[10]

Bush's scepticism may have been well founded. He had an old-fashioned, restrained style, and did not believe in excessive displays of zeal or ideology. And indeed he did win the presidency in 1988. But four years later he was defeated by the charismatic young Governor of Arkansas, Bill Clinton.

Clinton had 'the vision thing'. He showed his emotions. He felt people's pain. He told a story about 'a place called Hope', the town in Arkansas where he was born. He seemed to be interested in other people, and wanted to learn about their stories. It may have been schmaltzy, and subsequently undermined by his behaviour in office, but Clinton ultimately proved to be a popular president who would have been re-elected again in 2000 had the US constitution allowed such a thing to happen.

Bush's rejection of 'the vision thing' has come to stand as a warning to leaders not to underestimate the need to have a big and appealing story to tell followers. It does not necessarily have to be, nor should it be, a 'Grand Vision' (and we will say more about this word 'vision' in chapter 6). But describing the task in hand in an inspiring way is undoubtedly a core element of leadership.

Words into action

Describing is one thing, and doing is another. Words are useful but need to be directed towards action. Leaders cannot be pure theoreticians. What they say should prompt others to put plans into effect.

This is the danger of high-flown visionary utterances and over-ambitious mission statements. You can't do anything with them. They stand as superficially impressive words on a poster or on a pledge card. But they do not make anything happen. 'Leadership involves plumbing as well as poetry,' as the late James March, emeritus professor at Stanford's graduate school of business, said.[11]

So even as leaders succeed in explaining to their business or organization what matters now and what has to be done, they should make sure their words have follow through, and consequences.

There are two main ways leaders can achieve this. The first is to make sure that they are able to receive information as well as transmit it – that is, ensuring there is a real dialogue in the workplace and not merely a leadership monologue.

The second is for the leader to model the sort of behaviour he or she wants to see in others – so not just talking a good game, but actually playing it too. That is the topic we shall go on to discuss next.

Set an example (actions/behaviour)

One of the consequences of the modern obsession with leadership is that leaders' behaviour is studied more closely than ever. There was a time when leaders could be a bit more remote and unknown. They could stay behind the curtain like the Wizard of Oz.

But now the demand for transparency is strong. You had better get used to it if you want to lead. If you work closely with your people they will want access to you and expect to see you around the place. And even if you are not based in the same country you will have to travel regularly to see them in person: show up and show yourself.

Every breath you take – they'll be watching you. This is why the traditional wisdom about setting a good example with your behaviour is even more pertinent than it used to be. It really matters.

Be the change

How do you show up at work? And how do you behave? It would be wrong to expect other people to work harder than you do – you are getting the big bucks after all. So pay attention to your time-keeping and availability.

As a leader you set the tone as well as setting an example. So mood swings and excessive public displays of emotion should be avoided. If you start to panic don't be surprised if your people do too.

But, equally, if you want to avoid a long-hours culture, and genuinely believe that meaningful flexibility will help your business do better, then prove it. Don't adopt the 'first one in, last person out' approach beloved of some bosses. Don't send emails late at night or right through the weekend. Take the holiday that is due to you, and make the most of flexible working arrangements yourself. These are good examples to set, echoing Gandhi's famous phrase about being 'the change you want to see in the world'. Until the boss starts doing it, many people at all levels will not believe the organization is serious about changing the way people work. When in early 2018 the UK's minister responsible for promoting shared parental leave revealed that he would not in fact be taking advantage of the system when his new baby arrived there was much hilarity, of course. But also there was a sad recognition that this sort of paradox is all too common in working life. It's what you do, not what you say, that counts.

'Hello Seattle, I'm listening'

Dr Frasier Crane, Seattle's favourite on-air therapist, may or may not have meant it when he told the city's inhabitants that he was listening and interested in their affairs. But leaders cannot hide in a radio studio and merely pretend to listen. One of the most important examples a leader can set is being seen to listen actively and act on what he or she is told.

You may need to set up several listening channels to make it clear that you are serious. 'All hands' meetings can work, but are not the only option. Smaller groups ('brown bag lunches'), online discussion, even dreaded away-days – all these things can give people a chance to speak up. But that is just the first step. Consultation is one of the most abused words in management. A leader who claims to invite views but then ignores them is no leader. You must be seen to have listened. Even if you reject the advice you have received, at least say why you have done so. People will know that you were listening and may even respect the choice you have made.

Time to go

There is one other crucial example which leaders need to know how to set: when to step aside. Having fought for so long to reach the top, and quite possibly having enjoyed the ride, leaders can often overstay their welcome. They may fear being less busy or less relevant. They may worry about no longer being at the heart of things. But these are selfish and self-centred instincts. Part of the job of a leader is handing on an organization that is at least viable and preferably in better shape than when you took over. Believing your own hype about your success, your indispensability or infallibility will lead you astray.

Both Jack Welch and Jeff Immelt won plaudits at different times for their leadership at General Electric, the great US conglomerate. But both arguably stayed too long (Welch did twenty years at the top, and Immelt seventeen), delaying necessary change. Sir Terry Leahy led Tesco brilliantly for many years, but lost his touch when backing a doomed US venture. After he left, the business faced several years of difficulty which cannot be blamed solely on his successors. Things must have started going wrong while he was still at the top. And so on.

Sir John Parker, former chair of the mining group Anglo-American, put it bluntly in an interview with the *FT*: 'I have never, ever stayed long enough for any board to say: "It's time you moved on".'[12] Leave them wanting more.

Resign!

In the worst cases, when things have really gone badly wrong on your watch, when you are responsible, you should of course resign. There are not nearly enough prompt and timely resignations in business or in public life these days. People try to cling on, hide behind lawyers or PR advice, or hope to simply 'tough it out'. This is almost always a mistake. A swift, honourable resignation is something you can come back from. Being slowly and painfully forced from office after weeks of criticism is not.

Leaders are important. What they do is important. Have enough respect for the role and the people you lead to be conscious of how you act and how you come across. Don't take the credit for other people's work. Praise those who deserve it, in public. Criticize mainly in private. And when the time has come to walk away, go, and do not wait to be told. Leaving well is the final good example you need to set.

Have followers

It's quite simple really: if you don't have followers then you cannot be a leader. And by followers I don't mean people who have to report to you. They may sit under you in a hierarchy but that doesn't make you their leader. Employees choose to follow or not. If they are convinced by you and feel that their work is worthwhile they may make 'discretionary effort' – that is, they will bother.

'Employee engagement', as it is known, is hard to measure accurately and difficult to pin down, but you know it when you see it and experience it (whether as a customer or a colleague). Good managers may win some of that discretionary effort, and good leaders create the environment in which this is more likely to happen.

If you follow me

Gareth Jones and Rob Goffee asked the right question in their award-winning *Harvard Business Review* article 'Why should anyone be led by you?' (2000),[13] which they later expanded into an important book with the same title.[14] They avoided the pitfall of too much writing and research into leadership – being fixated on supposedly heroic individual figures – and instead thought about leadership from the point of view of those who were being led.

They spent a lot of time listening to people at work and finding out what they thought. They found that there were four essential qualities that people at work wanted their leaders to help create and build: community, authenticity, significance, and excitement.

Community matters, because a sense of belonging and shared identity helps bind a workforce together. Diversity alone may not necessarily deliver anything special, without inclusion. When a business or organization feels like a community you don't need so many rules or intrusive management supervision. People just know what to do, and set standards for each other as peers. A business that builds community will have a strong and hard-to-copy culture, which could give you a competitive advantage. So leaders need to think hard about what they are doing to build that sense of community.

Authenticity matters because people can spot a phoney boss from a hundred yards. Transparency and openness require leaders to show more of themselves, so the truth had better not be too unpleasant or unappealing. Leaders expect a lot from their people. In return, people at work want bosses to level with them, not to dissemble and to tell them a true story about where the organization is headed. This cannot be faked. Be authentic if you want to lead.

Significance matters because work should mean something. If you are asking for commitment and attention to detail then work must also have some variety and interest in it. Good leaders help people to understand why their work matters, and why it is meaningful – even if it might not necessarily appear that way at first. We have all heard that possibly too-good-to-be-true story about the man sweeping the floor at NASA headquarters who, when asked by President Kennedy what he was doing, said: 'I'm helping to put a man on the moon.' Whether this really happened or not, it makes a good point about people finding significance at work.

Excitement matters because, again, leaders expect a lot from people. Maybe excitement (or 'fun') at work seems too much to ask some of the time. But its opposite, clearly, is tedium. Which leader would want to instil boredom in his or her workforce? Bosses should not want their people to get bored, so they need to introduce some variety and allow workers to manage their own time as far as is possible. Where there is excitement there will also be greater enjoyment, engagement and productivity.

'There's no discouragement . . .'

Leaders win followers by inspiring people and encouraging them. Not everyone can be inspirational. Charisma is an over-rated quality – too often a short-lived burst or sugar rush of apparent excitement, followed by a let down and the question: 'What was that all about?' Deeds and character can inspire in the long term; words alone may not last.

But encouragement is something that any leader ought to be able to provide. Courage is the greatest of all the virtues, Dr Johnson said, as without courage it will not be possible to act. In a confusing and troubling world people need to be encouraged at work, and this is a central task for any leader. If you want people to follow you, encourage them.

This is something the seventeenth-century writer John Bunyan understood. His work *The Pilgrim's Progress* contains famous words which later were adapted to become one of the most popular of English hymns, 'He who would Valiant be', also known as 'To Be a pilgrim'.[15]

The hymn is all about the desire and commitment of someone who has chosen to follow a given path – in this case that of religious faith, of course. But the sentiments are striking whether you are a person of faith or not:

> There's no discouragement
> shall make him once relent
> his first avowed intent
> to be a pilgrim . . .
>
> Then fancies flee away!
> I'll fear not what men say,
> I'll labour night and day
> to be a pilgrim.

This is not to suggest that businesses and organizations should become cults, and that a cultish following is the mark of a great leader. Far from it. But it is that sense of commitment and enthusiasm that the best leaders can bring about in others.

Anyone aspiring to lead should ask themselves Goffee and Jones's question: why should anyone be led by you? You need to have a good answer. And a key part of that answer will show why someone should bother following you, and why that followership will last. When you make a big presentation to staff, and effectively say to your people 'follow me!', if no one moves a muscle something has gone wrong. This is an acid test for any leader. Look behind you. If there is nobody following then I am afraid you are no sort of leader at all.

Achieve results

Fine words butter no parsnips. In fact, you won't grow any parsnips at all without taking action and working to get a result. This is a key point to make about leadership, before we get too deeply involved in this discussion (or too intoxicated with fine phrase-making). Leadership must lead to something useful: tangible outcomes, improvement, results. If it does not then it is all talk, or performance art. Temporarily distracting, entertaining even, but ultimately useless.

This point may seem so basic as to be hardly worth making. And yet: how many supposedly 'great' leaders move on from their top job leaving a less than substantial track record behind them? How many business heroes are revealed to be ordinary mortals once they are no longer in post? To be a true leader you have to get important things done.

'What was that about?'

This is why there will not be a lot of speculation about what charisma is in this book, or how you could develop more of it. (Disappointed readers should turn away now.) Jim Collins, the author of *Good to Great*, told me once that he found charisma to be a remarkably uninteresting and almost irrelevant concept. 'If I'm enormously charismatic, I can convince you to do a lot of things because of the force of my personality,' Collins told me. 'But force of personality is not an argument . . . It's not facts, it's not evidence, it's not data . . . Charisma is irrelevant. It's not good or bad, it's irrelevant.'[16]

We see this borne out in politics as well as business. 'All political lives, unless they are cut off in midstream at a happy juncture, end in failure, because that is the nature of politics and of human affairs', Enoch Powell famously said.[17] Even once dominant, charismatic figures, such as Bill Clinton or Barack Obama, once they are no longer regularly on the big stage, can seem immediately diminished. As one sceptic asked at the end of the Clinton presidency: 'What was that about?' It was exciting while it lasted. But then what? The best leaders leave a lasting legacy.

Getting stuff done

Herb Kelleher, founder and former CEO of Southwestern Airlines in the US, insisted on a pragmatic commitment to action in building his business' ethos of customer service. He declared that strategy was over-rated, and that doing stuff was under-rated. 'Our strategy – do stuff,' he said.[18] (I promise to repeat this line at least once more before you get to the end of this book.)

This is what leaders need to transmit to their people through everything they say and do. If leaders are not 'action-centred', why would anyone else in the organization be? Churchill's 'action this day' instruction to colleagues is another example of this. Leaders should demand action, and results.

Milestones

One leader who has always impressed me with his commitment to action and results is Sir William Sargent, co-founder and chief executive of Framestore, the specialist visual effects company, which has worked on such award-winning movies as *Paddington* and *Gravity*.

The company has been going for over thirty years now, and has grown from having a handful of employees to over 600 with operations in London, New York, Los Angeles and Montreal. In November 2016, the business was sold to Chinese investors for £150m.

Sargent told me that he has never seen the point of making plans for the medium term. Life is too complicated, and the unexpected will turn up. Instead, he has always had two different time horizons in mind. First, the very short term and day to day: staying on top of projects and progress on a weekly and even daily basis, making sure that their film-maker clients' needs are being met.[19]

The second time horizon is the very long term. Every new client, every project and every piece of Framestore's work has to be consistent with what the firm is trying to achieve (world-class excellence in visual effects), and doing that high-quality work in the right way. Everything else in between those short-term project milestones and the very long term can be left to look after itself. As a plan it has turned out rather well. This is leadership based around purposeful action.

Results

'Judge me on results' is the motto of many a sports coach. And it's a fair method of assessment. Especially in a professional sport, where winning is just about everything, it's reasonable for a manager to hold on to a job while the results still look good. And when the losses start to stack up, no one can complain when they are shown the door.

This is not a bad model for any leader, in business or anywhere else, to adopt. You should and will be judged on your results. It follows that you need to make sure the targets you are aiming for make sense – that they are stretching and ambitious, but also not impossible to achieve or unrealistic.

This is where leaders really earn their money. The organization is looking to you for direction. People want to be engaged in meaningful activity. They need to know what results are expected of them, and how they should measure their success (or lack of it).

Do stuff

This is why Herb Kelleher's strategy of 'do stuff' is so helpful. (Told you there would be a second appearance. There may be a third.) Leaders probably worry a bit too much about strategy (we shall discuss this nonetheless important topic at greater length later on), and not enough about getting things done, or 'execution', as the slightly daunting business jargon term has it. It is a truism, and therefore true, that a business with a good enough strategy but excellent execution will beat a rival which has a far more ingenious strategy but feeble execution. Echoing the words of the old song, it's not what you do, but how you do it – and that's what gets results. Leaders should get results.

2:

WHAT DO BAD LEADERS GET WRONG?

It's all about them

The famous English football manager, Brian Clough – who did not lack self-confidence – was once chatting to the BBC sports correspondent, Pat Murphy, when Frank Sinatra's name came up in the conversation. 'That Sinatra, Patrick – he's met me, you know,' Clough said.[20]

Narcissism is a seemingly inevitable characteristic – or should that be 'symptom'? – of many of those who feel moved to lead. You can see why this might be so. When there is so much discussion about the personality of the leader, potential leaders are bound to worry and think a lot about themselves. And to some extent this is both natural and healthy, for reasons we set out in the introduction.

But where productive examination of the self tips into damaging obsession – or solipsism, the idea that 'I am all there really is' – then bad leaders and bad leadership are to be found. The sense that 'this is all about me' pervades every conversation and interaction with the boss.

The media and financial markets are partly to blame for encouraging narcissistic tendencies. We talk about complicated organizations through the personality of the boss. We imply that one human being, called CEO, can single-handedly change the destiny of a business. This is nonsense, of course, but it feeds the ego and self-importance of leaders. We should think about the workplace and organizations in a deeper, more sophisticated way. Otherwise we just make existing narcissism worse.

Analyse this

The anthropologist and psychoanalyst Michael Maccoby has written powerfully about both the good and bad aspects of narcissism. His *Harvard Business Review* article – 'Narcissistic leaders: the incredible pros, the inevitable cons' (2000) – won the McKinsey award for the being most influential HBR article of the year.[21] The bad things about narcissism are widely understood. As Maccoby wrote in his article:

> Freud recognized that there is a dark side to narcissism. Narcissists, he pointed out, are emotionally isolated and highly distrustful. Perceived threats can trigger rage. Achievements can feed feelings of grandiosity. That's why Freud thought narcissists were the hardest personality types to analyse ... Not surprisingly, most people think of narcissists in a primarily negative way. After all, Freud named the type after the mythical figure Narcissus, who died because of his pathological preoccupation with himself.

And here is Maccoby's taxonomy of narcissism:

> Narcissists are typically not comfortable with their own emotions. They listen only for the kind of information they seek. They don't learn easily from others. They don't like to teach but prefer to indoctrinate and make speeches. They dominate meetings with subordinates.

The result for the organization is greater internal competitiveness at a time when everyone is already under as much pressure as they can possibly stand. Perhaps the main problem is that the narcissist's faults tend to become even more pronounced as he becomes more successful.

However, Maccoby says, we should not underestimate the creative potential of what he calls 'productive narcissists'. He quotes Freud: 'People of this type impress others as being "personalities". They are especially suited to act as a support for others, to take on the role of leaders, and to give a fresh stimulus to cultural development or damage the established state of affairs.'

In Maccoby's view, productive narcissists are,

> . . . gifted and creative strategists who see the big picture and find meaning in the risky challenge of changing the world and leaving behind a legacy. Indeed, one reason we look to productive narcissists in times of great transition is that they have the audacity to push through the massive transformations that society periodically undertakes. Productive narcissists are not only risk takers willing to get the job done but also charmers who can convert the masses with their rhetoric. The danger is that narcissism can turn unproductive when, lacking self-knowledge and restraining anchors, narcissists become unrealistic dreamers. They nurture grand schemes and harbour the illusion that only circumstances or enemies block their success. This tendency toward grandiosity and distrust is the Achilles' heel of narcissists. Because of it, even brilliant narcissists can

come under suspicion for self-involvement, unpredicta-
bility, and – in extreme cases – paranoia.

The Donald

By now you will inevitably have been reminded of the person
whom we must still call, at the time of writing, President
Trump. It Is All About Him. According to the author Michael
Wolff (in his book *Fire and Fury*), Trump instructed his White
House staff to regard his presidency as a reality TV show
which he had to 'win' every day. Trump has spoken of getting
'great ratings' for his announcements and actions.[22] And he
deserves the credit, it seems, for anything good that ever
happens. It Is All Down To Him.

Trump is giving narcissism a very bad name. And he
provides encouragement to all bad leaders everywhere, in
politics or business, who may draw the conclusion that the
more outrageous and outlandish their behaviour is, the
better.

Leaders need to remember that it is not all about them.
They need to hire good people, delegate wisely, trust their
colleagues, and be a team player – even if they are also the
team leader. Work gets done by groups of people, not individuals. Leaders are important but they are not everything
and they are only rarely indispensable or irreplaceable.

Jury's out, for now

Michael Maccoby takes a more balanced view on narcissistic
leaders than many of us would. With Trump we are clearly
getting an extreme example. But all is not lost, just yet.
There might be a role for productive narcissists even now.

'Companies need leaders who do not try to anticipate the future so much as create it,' Maccoby says. 'But narcissistic leaders – even the most productive of them – can self-destruct and lead their organizations terribly astray.' This next sentence, the closing line of his article, was written almost twenty years ago, but it still rings true: 'For companies whose narcissistic leaders recognize their limitations, these will be the best of times. For other companies, these could turn out to be the worst.'

Disrupt to no good end

Restlessness can be quite a good quality for a leader to have, within reason. Settling for merely adequate results might gradually take a company down. Complacency is death. The Japanese concept of *kaizen* – continuous improvement – is not based on the idea of people turning up at work for a rest. Leadership means making sure that everyone is awake, alert and ready to perform.

Unfortunately, some leaders pick this notion of 'busyness' and turn it into something far less productive. Uncomfortable with calm and steady output, they seek chaos and confusion. And what a noxious gift the now greatly overused term of 'disruption' has been to bosses like this. They see themselves as the disruptor-in-chief.

Professor Clayton Christensen of Harvard Business School could have had no idea what the world would do with his concept of 'disruptive innovation', which is now over twenty years old.[23] Christensen was talking specifically about low-cost entrants to markets with new business models. He did not mean that disruption at all costs and at all times was necessarily a good idea. Too late. Now the way to get people's attention in meetings is to claim you have a disruptive idea, or that this or that business or area of activity is ripe for disruption ('Uber, but for [fill in gap]'). So one way for leaders to try and sound like they know what they are doing is to demand more disruption and to be a disruptive presence themselves.

This approach undermines colleagues while lending the speaker bogus authority. But not all disruptions are good. As long as there is chaos in the air, however, the insecure boss is happy, sowing confusion.

Initiative of the week

The same problems emerge during over-ambitious 'culture change' programmes. Converted to the belief that 'the only constant is change', some organizations latch onto a phrase or concept which for a time is supposed to be regarded as incredibly important, until the next one comes along to replace it. When your author worked at the BBC in the mid-1990s, it was decided that the journalistic test to be applied to stories was 'significance' – did this investigation really matter or not? It wasn't a bad thought. But after a time the organization moved on to the next big idea or theme.

Under another boss, Greg Dyke, the BBC committed to being 'the most creative organization in the world'. Staff were issued with yellow cards, such as those wielded by football referees, and were encouraged to 'cut the crap' and 'make it happen'.[24] These weren't necessarily stupid ideas either. But after subsequent turmoil at the BBC in the wake of the Iraq war the leadership changed again and new words and buzz phrases emerged. And so on.

Flavour of the month

Organizations get wise to this sort of thing. One seasoned consultant describes it this way: '"Oh yes, it's a priority," is what everybody says in the meetings. And then once the meeting is over and the boss has left the room . . . nothing.'

Inertia is a powerful force, and the organization can resist, actively and passively. The latest call for 'agility' from the workforce is likely to meet a similar fate. Of course, no one can object to the idea of being flexible and adapting to meet the demands of the day. In practice, however, this can be hard to pull off. The other point about 'continuous improvement' is that it will probably involve only modest, perhaps even tiny adjustments. The sort of lasting change that makes a difference will be embedded gradually over time, not rushed in with a big bang approach. Disruption is the enemy of continuous improvement. It makes too much noise and leaves too much of a mess.

Continuity and change

Bad leaders are all change and no continuity. You need both. One of the tricks of leadership is knowing when to shake things up a bit (ok, 'disrupt', if you must), and when to allow people to get on with their work undisturbed.

Another reason why Donald Trump sets such a bad example as a leader is that he clearly relishes the daily disruption of declaring that black is white and upending relationships, even though it makes for chaos and confusion in the most important elected office in the world. As David Remnick, editor of the *New Yorker*, wrote in his magazine: 'Trump has created a poisonous culture in his administration that is not only doing great damage to the country but is also destroying itself.'[25]

He is a stress infector: nobody can be sure of where they stand with him from one day to the next. He was fortunate to inherit a strong and growing economy. We must hope we do not get to find out how he would react in a genuine crisis or moment of economic collapse. But it is appalling that the 'leader of the free world' models this sort of disruptive behaviour. If you are wondering how to act as a leader, ask yourself: what would Donald do? And then do the opposite of that.

The cure

The antidote to this sort of restlessness is to find some trusted colleagues and advisers who will tell you the truth. Do not take decisions on your own. Test your thinking. Question your prejudices and biases. It could be good to have a certain impatience with delays and muddle, and urge the organization on to move quicker. But that urgency also has to be patient. As John Kotter, emeritus professor at Harvard Business School, and expert on change, says in his book *A Sense of Urgency*, leaders could demonstrate this by 'acting each day with a sense of urgency but having a realistic view of time. It means recognizing that five years may be needed to attain important and ambitious goals, and yet coming to work each day committed to finding every opportunity to make progress toward those goals.'[26]

Deny the truth

'I don't want to be surrounded by yes men,' the Hollywood mogul Samuel Goldwyn is supposed to have said. 'I want people who'll disagree with me, even if it costs them their jobs.'[27]

Maybe Goldwyn was joking. Maybe he never even really said it. But the line captures the paradox about the difficulty of getting tough (aka 'career-limiting') messages through to the boss. There is quite an art to it which many of us never truly master.

There's a reason why it can be hard to deliver the bad news. Bad leaders try to shut out the truth. They can't – won't – hear it. This can be down to their insecurity. It could be that they have massive optimism bias and simply cannot cope with inconvenient facts. The boss may have a crude belief in the language of 'winning', and simply deny that anything bad is ever happening.

Whistle-blowers come to the fore where bad leaders are trying to suppress the truth. It is a pretty sure sign that something has gone wrong in the culture and practice of a business if a whistle-blower feels the need to step forward. But the cult-like nature of organizations where certain truths cannot be told is powerful, resilient and resists attempts to change it. In such circumstances, truth-tellers are looked on as a virus that has to be eradicated before it can infect everybody else, giving them a greater appetite for truth.

This is why bad leadership can be so toxic and so destructive for the culture of organizations. What do we see happening to whistle-blowers again and again? They are marginalized, they are shut out, they are rubbished and they are belittled. They are bullied until they shut up or go away. Yes, whistle-blowers can be paid-up 'awkward squad' members, such as Paul Moore at HBOS, the compliance officer who tried to warn bosses that crazy loans were being written. It is easy to discount people as 'oddballs' and 'whingers' if you do not like what they are telling you.[28]

Internal warning systems – safe channels – should be in place to allow those with important bad news to speak up. But this happens all too rarely. The result? Scandals and corporate collapses. The truth comes out in the end, but too late to save the business. So good leaders do not shoot messengers but seek out the bad and difficult news (see page 38).

Fake news

This is just one of the ways in which Donald Trump (yes, him again) embodies bad leadership. Trump seems psychologically incapable of admitting that anything bad has happened during his presidency, and if it has, it must have been the fault of some other guy. He also seeks to claim credit for developments – improved air traffic safety, for example – which have had absolutely nothing to do with him.

His press spokesman was not allowed to admit that Barack Obama's inauguration had drawn bigger crowds than Trump's. Hillary Clinton only got three million more votes than Trump 'because of fraud'. President Obama had apparently ordered that Trump's phones be tapped (he didn't). And so on. The person who has popularized the dreadful term 'fake news' is of course the biggest source of the stuff himself.

This is poisonous, and harmful to public life both in the US and further afield. His is the most prominent, perhaps the most important leadership job in the world. And he is setting an abysmal example.

Over 1,500 years ago, St Augustine wrote: 'When regard for truth has been broken down, or even slightly weakened, all things will remain doubtful'.[29] Trump's sweeping dismissal of any data he doesn't like as 'fake news' has been a crudely effective trick. We have all fallen for it to some extent. Some American journalists are doing their best to scrutinize the Trump technique, but it is an exhausting and unrewarding process, not helped by the shameful acquiescence and collaboration of some Republican politicians and one or two mainstream media outlets

The Trump presidency has constituted a challenge to Enlightenment values and civilized ideals. We must hope the damaging effects do not prove permanent. But if you want an example of a bad leader trying to shut out the truth you need look no further.

Taming the truth deniers

Is there anything we can do to tame, retrain or prevent truth-denying leaders from doing further harm to the organizations they lead? It is, sadly, a bit late once they have already got to the top. As Professor Jeffrey Pfeffer of Stanford University's graduate school of business has observed, it is naive to expect bad people to change once they get the top job, especially if their bad behaviour has helped to get them there.[30]

And, tough though it is to admit it, some of these toxic leaders can appear to succeed, at least in the short term. As Pfeffer told Forbes in 2015: 'We need to understand – and then do something about – the disconnect between the leaders and companies we honour on the most admired lists and the companies that are truly great places to work with healthy workplaces. The fact that admired leaders and companies can be truly toxic workplaces strikes me as a major reason why so many people are in abusive, bullying, stressful work environments.'[31]

The longer-term solution is for better people to get into leadership positions and start to change the workplace cultures they preside over. But this takes time. And it requires existing leaders to spot the potential of future leaders and promote them, which may not happen if the current regime feels threatened by the new wave of people coming through.

This is why people leave organizations, of course, and go and start their own businesses, having given up on or rejected the culture in which they are working. But even a healthy 'exit interview' may reveal truths that are not allowed to be shared openly with the boss. And so the cycle continues, until, we hope, creative destruction and natural selection deal with the doomed entity.

They are indecisive

Flip-flop. Flip-flop. No, not an advertisement for footwear. This is the lethal accusation made against politicians and business leaders who seem to change their mind too often. When the presidential candidate John Kerry tried to explain why he had reversed his earlier position on voting for military spending in 2003 he got into terrible trouble. 'I actually did vote for the $87 billion before I voted against it,' he said, thus creating one of the all-time famous political gaffes.[32]

In the UK flip-flopping is known as performing a U-turn. To accuse a leader of carrying out a U-turn is seen one of the most powerful criticisms you can make. The longevity of this insult is testament to the remarkable endurance of Margaret Thatcher's reputation, for it was she who first popularized it.

It was October 1980, and Mrs Thatcher was heading to her Conservative party conference in Brighton in some political difficulty. She had been prime minister for eighteen months, and the UK economy was struggling. Unemployment was rising fast, as was her unpopularity.

Pundits predicted that, like Edward Heath before her, Mrs Thatcher would buckle under the pressure and reverse some tough policy decisions. But, in a now famous – some would say infamous – passage in her speech, she said this: 'To those waiting with bated breath for that favourite media catchphrase, the U-turn, I have only one thing to say: you turn if you want to. The lady's not for turning!'[33]

And so a legend, or myth, was born, and almost forty years later to be accused of U-turning remains a deadly danger.

We can argue that this is regrettable – that in reality, circumstances change and therefore decisions need to change too. And that is true. But it is also true that leaders cannot afford to be seen as indecisive and uncertain. 'For if the trumpet give an uncertain sound, who shall prepare himself to the battle?' as St Paul wrote in his first letter to the Corinthians[34]

Make your mind up time

Of course, taking decisions isn't always easy. This is one of the reasons why leaders get paid more. If a manager brings a dilemma to his or her boss for adjudication it's because the more junior executive needs the authority of the more senior one to act. 'By the time something reaches my desk, that means it's really hard. Because if it were easy, somebody else would have made the decision and somebody else would have solved it,' as President Obama said.[35]

Professor Michael Useem, director of the Center for Leadership and Change Management at Wharton business school in Philadelphia, wrote a book about the difficulty of taking decisions called *The Go Point: When It's Time to Decide – Knowing What to Do and When to Do It*.[36] In an interview about the book he explained why leaders can be afflicted by indecision, and suggested ways of dealing with it.[37]

The problem, he said, was that 'people in mid-level office – sometimes in high office – are just not great at knowing when to pull the trigger, and how to pull it when they do . . . decision making as a skill is learned really by making decisions.' And, of course, 'Life is really just one decision after another: none easy.'

These challenges are not restricted to business leaders. 'If you carry responsibility in a church, a school, synagogue, a foundation, a government agency, from 9am to 5pm, your leadership often comes down to decision making,' Professor Useem said.

Who trains leaders well in the business of taking decisions? Unsurprisingly, Useem mentioned the military, and in particular the US Marine Corps.

The Marine Corps, he said, trains officers in the art of combat, knowing that the marines are often first in and the first to get out. 'The Marine Corps creates a culture where indecision is failure,' he said. '"Make a decision" is the adage that Marine Corps officers are taught.'

How should you know when it is the right moment to make a decision? You will never have 'perfect information' –

all the knowledge you might want to have before acting. 'The Marine Corps talks 70 per cent,' Useem said. 'When you're 70 per cent confident people are 70 per cent on board, go. See where you are in that spectrum and make certain you don't go too early, but don't go too late.'

The considered alternative to hasty action is sometimes called 'maximum optionality'. It characterized the approach of the former US Treasury Secretary Robert Rubin. His view was that he wanted to make a decision only when it had to be decided, and he wanted to get as much input as possible beforehand. According to Professor Useem he was known for saying: 'We're just not going to make that decision now. We're going to make it when we have to make it.'

The obvious risk here is that you simply put off decisions indefinitely – 'analysis paralysis' – and miss the right moment to take them. Professor Useem advises: 'Make certain you have a "bias for action". That is, if there's a moment when decisions should be made, be ready to make them. Don't shoot from the hip, but if it's a moment where your leadership is on the line . . .'

'Muttley, do something!'

Dick Dastardly, the fiendish yet unlucky baddie from the popular cartoon series *Wacky Races*, used to command his put-upon dog Muttley to 'do something!' when the situation was truly dire. It turns out that this is quite good advice, some of the time.

If you saw the remarkable documentary film *Touching the Void*, about Joe Simpson and Simon Yates' doomed mountaineering expedition in the Peruvian Andes, you will know the value of action.

Simpson had broken his leg and, in the confusion of their descent from the summit, had had his rope cut by his partner. This had been done with the best of intentions – to try and save them both. Simpson became almost delirious with dehydration, hunger and tiredness. But even in his exhausted state he recognized that he had to take action. He could have waited to try and come up with the perfect solution to his plight. But he knew he would have died before working that out. Instead, he decided simply to 'do something!' and then react to what happened as a result.

Miraculously he made it back to base camp. He got out alive to tell the tale.

A learned skill

We can be quite hard on indecisive ditherers and U-turners. Sometimes we are right to be harsh. But you only really get better at decision making by doing more of it – a point made nicely by this imagined dialogue by the psychology department at the University of Pennsylvania:

> Q: What is the secret of your success?
> A: Two words.
> Q: What are they?
> A: Right decisions.
> Q: How do you make right decisions?
> A: One word.
> Q: What is that?
> A: Experience.
> Q: How do you get experience?
> A: Two words.
> Q: What are they?
> A: Wrong decisions.[38]

3:

WHAT DO GOOD LEADERS GET RIGHT?

Confront the brutal facts (realism)

'How did you go bankrupt?' Bill asked.

'Two ways,' Mike said. 'Gradually and then suddenly.'

'What brought it on?'

'Friends,' said Mike. 'I had a lot of friends. False friends. Then I had creditors, too.'

—Ernest Hemingway, *The Sun Also Rises* [39]

'Start from where you are' runs the traditional advice. Where else should you start, you might ask. But implicit in that advice is the idea that you need to recognize the reality of the situation you find yourself in.

Good leaders do this. They do not indulge in wishful thinking. They do not flatter their organizations with empty, feel-good chat. This is what can lead to the sort of gradual, almost imperceptible decline hinted at in the Hemingway passage quoted above.

The phrase 'confront the brutal facts' was popularized by the management guru Jim Collins in his bestseller *Good to Great*.[40] But he in turn took the phrase from a remarkable American war hero, Admiral Jim Stockdale, who was held prisoner in the 'Hanoi Hilton' during the Vietnam War for eight years, between 1965 and 1973.

During his incarceration Stockdale was tortured over twenty times. For his book Collins asked him how had faced up to his appalling circumstances and shown the resilience to survive.

'I never lost faith in the end of the story,' Stockdale told him. 'I never doubted not only that I would get out, but also that I would prevail in the end and turn the experience into the defining event of my life, which in retrospect, I would not trade.'

And then Collins asked him: 'Who didn't make it out?'

'Oh, that's easy,' Stockdale replied. 'The optimists.'

This answer threw Collins completely. Wasn't this a contradiction of what he had just said about not losing faith? Not really. The next answer explained all, and thus was 'the Stockdale paradox', as Collins called it, born:

> The optimists. Oh, they were the ones who said, 'We're going to be out by Christmas.' And Christmas would come, and Christmas would go. Then they'd say, 'We're going to be out by Easter.' And Easter would come, and Easter would go. And then Thanksgiving, and then it would be Christmas again. And they died of a broken heart. This is a very important lesson. You must never confuse faith that you will prevail in the end – which you can never afford to lose – with the discipline to confront the most brutal facts of your current reality, whatever they might be.'

It was Hemingway's friend and contemporary, F Scott Fitzgerald, who observed that the finest minds were able to hold two contradictory ideas in their heads at the same time. The Stockdale paradox seems to be an example of this. Keep faith that you can succeed. But do not flinch from the reality of your current position, no matter how grim it might be.

Infinite variety

What are the kinds of facts that leaders choose to ignore, or simply fail to recognize, thus helping to drag their organization down into trouble?

First, bosses may mistakenly believe they have 'cracked it', and that their success will be permanent. There was a time, two decades ago, when the UK retailer Marks and Spencer seemed to occupy a place of unshakeable dominance on the British high street. It generated profits of £1 billion for the first time around then, a previously unimaginable landmark. The M&S name was a byword for the sort of affordable quality the great mass of consumers wanted. And the business held a special place in the nation's affections.

But this did not last. 'Fast fashion' and high-end retailers both ate into M&S' once impenetrable market position. It was dominant no more. But the truth was this eventuality could have been foreseen with tougher-minded leadership.

A second risk is for leaders and their leadership teams to believe their own hype. Lord (John) Browne was known as 'the Sun King' as BP grew by acquisition in the late 1990s and into the new millennium. It seemed to be an all-conquering beast. BP could apparently do no wrong. But the company was in fact over-stretched, its core engineering competence no longer held sway, and disasters in Alaska, Texas City and the Gulf of Mexico cost the firm tens of billions and its reputation for excellence. Bad news and warnings had not got through to the top. Brutal facts were not confronted until it was far too late.

A third way of ignoring brutal facts is simply not to recognize the way in which the word is changing. The obvious example of this is Kodak, which had indeed started to develop digital camera technology but did not pursue it, believing that film was somehow here to stay. The company failed to invest in digital in order to protect its film business. But the plan failed, and, although Kodak finally and belatedly entered the digital camera business, in 2012 it filed for chapter 11 bankruptcy. Today Kodak is a vastly smaller digital-imaging company employing around 6,000 people globally, down from over 140,000 in the mid-1980s.

A fourth brutal fact is a basic lack of cash, a fate which befell the builder and outsourced service provider Carillion in early 2018. Contracts were still being written and business was still being run. But the company had very little cash, large debts and a growing pension fund deficit. The profit margins on its public sector contracts in particular were tiny. Still the company kept paying dividends to shareholders, with borrowed money. But the debts grew too big and the business collapsed. How did Carillion go bankrupt, you ask? Two ways: gradually, and then suddenly.

Look in the mirror and look at the facts

The truth can hurt. It can also be dealt with. Good leaders will not shield their organizations from the truth, but will explain convincingly how it can be faced up to. But only leaders can do this. If they deny the truth, or keep it out of the boardroom, the consequences will be bleak.

This is why, as a leader, you need to get real and confront

the brutal facts. After all, if you can keep your head when all about you are losing theirs you've probably failed to grasp the seriousness of the situation.

Keep it simple

People are busy. Very busy. They lack 'bandwidth'. They lack energy and goodwill too, some of the time. It follows that leaders have very little time in which to make an impression and to get their message through.

Complexity is the enemy of leaders who want their people to understand what the business is trying to achieve. This is what AG Lafley, the former chief executive of Procter and Gamble, was getting at when he said that he tried to keep his communication with the business *'Sesame Street simple'*.

This was not a patronizing comment, nor a suggestion that his employees needed remedial help with their reading, writing and counting. In fact, he was showing his people respect. They had far better things to do, he recognized, than listen to the boss. Thinking about how to do their job better was not necessarily their top priority in life.

Bob Sutton, professor of organizational behaviour at Stanford's graduate school of business, wrote approvingly of Lafley's approach after seeing him give a talk to a group of executives. It struck a chord with him, because the Lafley style embodied what he and fellow Stanford professor Jeffrey Pfeffer had been writing about in their book *The Knowing-Doing Gap*. Wiser and more effective executives pick just a few simple messages and repeat them over and over again until people throughout the organization internalize them and use them to guide action. Constantly changing messages leads to the "flavour of the month problem", where people don't act on the current message because they have learned that, if they wait a few months (or days), the message will change. Managers in such organizations become very skilled at talking as if they are acting on the flavour of the month, but not actually doing the thing that senior executives are pushing at the moment. And making things overly complicated may make the senior executives seem smart and feel smart, but if a message is too complicated to understand, it is also means that the implications for action are impossible to understand as well.[41]

Does this sound like somewhere you have worked in the past, or where you are working now? We have all been there.

Why are you here?

The research firm Gallup has a twelve-question employee engagement survey, often referred to as the Gallup Q12, which attempts to unearth levels of engagement but also the quality of working life experienced by respondents. Question number one is: 'Do you know what is expected of you at work?' Seasoned HR professionals will tell you that this question alone can tell you a lot about the quality of leadership in a business or organization. Leaders who have kept up a simple but persistent (and consistent) message will register better scores. Those who have confused their organization or over-complicated their message will find that the number of employees answering 'no' to this question will be large.

This is pretty basic stuff – but the Gallup scores tell their own story. In the US, for example, only 33 per cent of employees are engaged at work. In the world's best businesses, Gallup says, that figure is as high as 70 per cent. In other words, 67 per cent of US workers are either 'not engaged' at work (51 per cent) or, worse, are 'actively disengaged' (16 per cent).

This sounds like a complicated problem – and it is. But part of the answer to this is simplicity. And when you consider that the world's leading HR guru, Dave Ulrich, has estimated with colleagues that employees need to hear a management message ten times, in various forms and media channels, before really registering it, you can see the need for both simplicity and consistency in what leaders say to their people.

There is too much going on in people's lives, and their time is too short to waste it with distractions, vagueness and complexity. It's a competitive world out there. If you want to survive you have to keep things simple. And if you think this last sentence repeats a point made earlier in this chapter, you're right. Feel lucky that you won't have to hear it ten times in three pages.

Survival

We shall talk a bit more, inevitably, about Winston Churchill later on in the book, in chapter 7. But first it is worth considering his take on the need for simplicity at a time of deep crisis. One of his early steps as war leader was to call for much shorter and simpler documents from his staff.

'To do our work, we all have to read a mass of papers,' he wrote in August 1940. 'Nearly all of them are far too long. This wastes time, while energy has to be spent in looking for the essential points.'

He concluded: 'Reports drawn up on the lines I propose may at first seem rough as compared with the flat surface of officialese jargon. But the saving in time will be great, while the discipline of setting out the real points concisely will prove an aid to clearer thinking.'[42]

Churchill had already displayed this kind of directness and simplicity in his first speech to the House of Commons as prime minister, on 13 May 1940. With the eyes of the country on him, he set out his stall, which proved an effective rallying cry for a nation standing alone and in peril: 'You ask, "what is our aim?" I can answer in one word: victory. Victory at all costs – victory in spite of all terror – victory, however long and hard the road may be, for without victory there is no survival.'[43]

Ok, so not every boss in peacetime faces such intense challenges as a great war leader. But there is still a clear lesson to be learned here by anyone who seeks to lead. Keep it simple. Keep it simple. Keep it simple.

Aim high

A leader, said Napoleon, is 'a dealer in hope'. 'So are bookies,' observed the American writer Michael Maccoby.[44] Point taken. But if we are talking about 'Hope' with a capital H, then that is certainly something that leaders need to inspire and provide.

Who wants a pessimist for a boss? Now, it may be that

guarded realism is a useful quality for a leader (or a leadership team) to have. One reason why leadership is ultimately a team activity is that you need a balance of perspectives at the top. A top team full of boundless optimists will lead to disaster, while if the pessimism factor is too high opportunities will be missed. And to expect one human being to maintain precisely the right balance between optimism and pessimism at all times is unrealistic.

But leadership, collectively, should mean aiming high. It should mean letting the organization know that the business has big expectations of what you can all achieve together. To some extent, leaders need to give a bit of house-room to their optimism bias, while remaining conscious at all times that this is what they are doing.

Confidence in confidence

'What's the best level of confidence?' asks Professor Phil Rosenzweig of the IMD business school in Lausanne in his book *Left Brain, Right Stuff – How leaders make winning decisions*. 'An amount that inspires us to do our best, but not so much that we become complacent, or take success for granted, or otherwise neglect what it takes to achieve high performance.'[45]

Professor Rosenzweig is one of the canniest observers of the realities of business that I know. (If you haven't read his essential *The Halo Effect* on the myths and delusions of business life then please do so.)[46] Business is a competition, he argues, which means that relative performance is crucial. He makes this important point about confidence and aiming high: 'When performance is relative the desired level of confidence can only be understood in the context of competition.

What's the best level of confidence? It's what we need to do better than our rivals,' he writes. There is nothing wrong in aiming high – or at least aiming higher than those around us. In fact it is important to do so.

So those who worry about alleged over-confidence may be making a big mistake, he argues. 'In much of our lives, where we can exert control and influence outcomes, what seems to be an exaggerated level of confidence may be useful; and when we add the need to outperform rivals, such a level of confidence may even be essential.'

Leadership as performance

A once fashionable concept in business was that leaders needed to aim for 'Big Hairy Audacious Goals', or BHAGs. That idea can be taken too far. Surrealism may have inspired interesting works of art but is not a good basis for disciplined leadership. Leaders should be rooted in reality. 'Keep your eyes on the stars but your feet on the ground,' as Teddy Roosevelt liked to say.

But aiming high, and being seen to aim high, is part of the necessary behavioural repertoire of the successful leader. People are watching. They will notice what standards you accept and which you don't. They will notice what behaviour gets rewarded, who gets promoted and who doesn't. They will see how ambitious and determined you are. In this sense, leadership is a public performance. In an age of increasing transparency it is hard to see it being anything else.

How should a leader show that he or she is aiming high? It is partly a matter of tone, of course. The messages you send out should be positive. Realistic, yes, but optimistic. And there should be frequent communication, in good times and bad. People need to hear from you and know what you are thinking.

Being accessible, showing up at team meetings to listen actively, taking on the difficult questions, offering a persuasive way forward: these are all parts of transmitting your aspirations for the organization. You have to be seen to care. If you don't care why on earth should anybody else?

Setbacks will occur. They have to be ridden out and recovered from. Avoid mood swings, and certainly hide any temporary bouts of despair from public view. Save that for bedtime. The next day you have to bounce back in, ready to lead again. Which does not mean hiding the truth from your team if things are really bad. You cannot lie. But equally you should not be adding to people's anxiety by betraying your doubts and dragging the mood down. Aiming high means constantly looking for positive steps to take to get you out of difficulty.

Positive thinking

Reckless optimism is irresponsible. There have been too many corporate failures based on wishful thinking to list them all here. But judicious, measured optimism is the leaders' best friend. It is a renewable resource. It is contagious. Be a cheerful leader and a happy warrior. And keep that aim high.

Even if he never uttered them, these words often attributed to Michelangelo ring true: 'The greater danger for most of us lies not in setting our aim too high and falling short; but in setting our aim too low, and achieving our mark.'

Good leaders do not settle for permanently adequate or good enough results. They want more, for the organization they lead as well as for themselves.

Keep learning

We need to make sure that our businesses and institutions are 'learning organizations', it is often said. Knowledge needs to be managed like an asset, and cherished like a resource. But what if the person at the top has forgotten how to learn? Can a business be a learning organization if the leadership has given up on learning? The chances are slim.

Satya Nadella, CEO of Microsoft, says it is his appetite for learning that has been crucial to him in his career. 'It's fascinating how we [always] think that burning ambition early on is what drives you,' he said in an interview at the Wharton business school. 'I think what I had, though, was some curiosity, and that's what sustained me in the long run.'[47]

Good leaders know that knowledge must flow as freely as possible through the organization. Transparency is not just a buzzword. It describes an approach to business that says: we have nothing (or very little) to hide, we all have something to learn from each other, and in particular relevant information from the front line – customers – needs to get through to the top fast.

Leaders should want to learn. The threshold to the CEO's office is not a finishing line. The work has to carry on, with attitudes and ideas being challenged and renewed all the time. If leadership is partly a question of recognizing how the world is changing, and adapting behaviour and decisions to fit that changing world, then the ability and appetite to learn are crucial leadership capabilities.

Fast Company

The American journalist Bill Taylor co-founded the influential business magazine *Fast Company* over twenty years ago. The magazine captured a moment of change in approaches to leadership and management. Taylor himself went on to become a highly regarded business commentator.

He has spoken very well on the need for leaders to keep learning in one of his 'Briefly Brilliant' video talks. He explains why leadership is all about managing change, and why to do that effectively leaders have to keep learning. 'The work of making deep-seated meaningful change,' he says, 'has become the defining work of our time . . . as leaders you have to create the conditions where people can work as distinctively as you hope to compete.'[48]

He asks this question of leaders and wannabe leaders: 'Are you determined, as a person trying to make sense of an uncertain and tumultuous world, to be sure that what you know doesn't limit what you can imagine?'

He explains why this is so important:

One of the occupational hazards for leaders, especially in periods of great change, is what I think of as the paradox of expertise. The longer you have worked in a field, the more accomplished you are, the harder it can be to see new patterns, new dangers, new possibilities. All too often, without ever intending it, we let what we know limit what we can imagine. Which is why the best leaders are the most insatiable learners . . . they are determined to stay interested: interested in big ideas, interested in little surprises, interested in the enduring mission of the enterprise and all new ways to bring that mission to life.

And he ends with this further challenge:

The question facing every leader and every organization engaged in change is: am I as a person learning as fast as the world is changing? Remember: when it comes to making change the ultimate challenge is not to out-muscle or even out-hustle the competition. It's to out-think the competition. And if you as a leader are determined to keep learning as fast as the world is changing you've got the best chance to out-think the competition.

Curiouser and curiouser

Walter Isaacson, the biographer of Leonardo da Vinci, says it was the artist's insatiable desire to learn more that helped him become so creative. His ambition was 'to learn everything you wanted about anything you wanted,' he explained in another Wharton interview. 'We could still be a little bit more like that. We silo ourselves too much. We specialize too much . . . just stay curious about everything.'

Leonardo makes a list every day of what he wants to learn. 'Why is the sky blue?' It's the things you and I asked when we were 10, but we outgrow our wonder years . . . It's not because he needs it to paint a painting. He needs it because he's Leonardo, and he just wants to know everything you can possibly know about everything that could be known.'[49]

Leaders who learn

Who are the role model CEOs who have shown this appetite for learning? Tesco's success in the 1990s was built on an appetite for data led by then CEO Terry Leahy and the Dunn-humby team, who introduced the Tesco Clubcard. This vital leap forward for the business was mocked at the time by rivals. But embracing new technology helped Tesco build a lead which lasted for two decades. They also improved their supply chain technology at the same time. This was led from the top by someone with an appetite for learning. Para-doxically, Tesco came unstuck when they failed to learn from the failures of others (the ill-advised expansion into the US with the Fresh and Easy chain).

At Unilever, Paul Polman insisted that the whole business must adapt the latest thinking and technology in terms of using fewer resources and being more sustainable. He announced the 'Big Hairy Audacious Goal' of doubling profitability and halving the use of raw materials over the past decade – and the company is well on the way to managing it.

At Rolls-Royce, Warren East has led a huge re-engineering of the company's ageing logistics operation. This was a brave move which had been put off for years. But by grasping this nettle and modernizing their systems, the company has saved many millions of pounds and won new lucrative contracts, finally cutting losses and returning to profitability. In a world of 'power by the hour' service contracts the company needed urgently to become more efficient.

At Amazon, Jeff Bezos is utterly relentless in his search for new ideas, experimentation and learning. 'It's always Day One' is a cliché at the firm – meaning the company must never get stale, must never settle for what it has achieved. 'Day Two is stasis. Followed by irrelevance. Followed by excruciating, painful decline. Followed by death. And that is why it is always Day One,' Bezos has said.[50] There is constant experimentation at Amazon, much of which customers may never notice, but the result is a leaner organization with lower prices (and tough working conditions for staff . . . but that is another story).

Satya Nadella says he's tried to change Microsoft from a 'know-it-all' to a 'learn-it-all' company. He agrees with Bill Taylor's 'paradox of expertise' that when a company has done well it can believe it has mastered everything. The 'learn-it-all' mentality is vital. 'That applies to CEOs and companies [too],' he says. 'I think it has been a helpful cultural metaphor for us.'[51]

And lastly – Her Majesty Queen Elizabeth II. The British royal family was shocked by the extent of its unpopularity, exposed when Diana, Princess of Wales died in 1997. Over the following twenty years, the Windsors engaged in a process of 'imperceptible change', which has led to their current huge popularity. The Queen herself was prepared to learn, to adapt and move on. It has been a remarkable example of leadership from someone who was neither too elevated nor too venerable to carry on learning.

4:

WHERE ARE YOU AND WHAT ARE YOU TRYING TO DO?

Start-ups

Ah, the thrill of the new! The blank page. The fresh start. Leaders need to display judicious, tempered optimism for much of the time. But woe to the business leader who can't be just a bit too enthusiastic at the start of something new.

Leading a start-up requires fierce energy, of course. Why would anyone tag along on a risky new venture if the founder doesn't seem to be excited about it? Belief cannot be faked when there is only a handful of colleagues working closely together. The leader will be watched, and you are going to be spending a lot of time in each other's company. The start-up team needs to know that you are serious about the tasks ahead. So be open about your enthusiastic commitment to the work. Don't hide it away – show it and share it.

But positive energy will be merely wishful thinking if certain start-up disciplines are not adhered to. Scott Anthony explained in his 2014 book *The First Mile* that there are several steps to be followed to keep a start-up on track.

This moment calls for DEFT leadership, he argued. The acronym stands for:

Document an idea to help surface hidden assumptions

Evaluate that idea from multiple angles

Focus on the most critical strategic uncertainties

Test rigorously and adapt quickly[52]

Leaders of start-ups must be clear thinkers. So this first stage of 'documenting the idea' calls for logic and lucidity. Clearly, a start-up inhabits the world of that over-used (or misused) word, innovation. (Not everything that seems new, or newish, might really be an innovation. And there is a difference between invention – finding or thinking of something new – and turning that idea into a real business or future revenue stream.)

Scott Anthony argues that a successful innovation usually has three central characteristics:

It meets a need

The idea is deliverable

It must be viable and sustainable

He then builds on this to list a further twenty-seven questions which the start-up leader ought to be able to answer about the start-up idea. These include: Who is the customer? What is the essence of the idea? What are the most likely revenue streams? What is the cost of earning those revenues? What partnerships will you need to form? Who is on the team? And so on (there's another twenty-one questions but you'll have to buy his book to see what they are).

Having thus documented the start-up idea thoroughly, you may then proceed to evaluate the idea, focus on the challenges you will face and then test the idea in practice and adapt where necessary. All this has to be led by the start-up leader – confidently, vigorously and competently.

Slings and arrows

And yet. Nothing will go truly to plan. Planning is essential, as General Eisenhower said, but plans are useless. Another predictable aspect of the life of a start-up leader is that things are going to go wrong, unpredictably. You will have to adapt your style and approach to meet the needs of the moment.

Money may be tight. The market may not respond in the way you imagined it would. Distribution, supply chains and the business cycle may all prove problematic. Colleagues will lose faith, be argumentative or maybe just leave. Others may lose their nerve. All these dramas, and more, lie in wait.

So the leader of a start-up has to maintain a certain outward calm even when things look bad. Mood swings and anxiety cannot be allowed to take hold. Indeed, it is precisely when others are losing heart that the steadiness of the leader should come to the fore.

Start with the end in mind

Success is a nicer problem to have. But it could also lead you astray. Over-confidence could set in. You may try to grow too fast, scaling up too quickly and allowing the cost base to grow unsustainably. One way to guard against early-onset hubris is to start your new venture with an ambitious but credible goal in mind. Think years, decades even, rather than weeks and months. This will help you ride out the early triumphs and disasters that might otherwise have derailed you.

Time-limited

Not every leader is suited to every role, to every leadership situation. If you are the company founder you may have a very clear idea of what you want the business to be. But a year or two in, will you still be the right person to lead it? Maybe you are more of an inventor/entrepreneur type, rather than a business administrator. Start-ups, not long-term business building, may be your thing.

Take honest advice from the people who know you best – preferably the team itself as well as investors or friends. Having got up and running, do they now need a different type of leadership, and a different type of leader? Recognizing what stage of development and maturity your business has reached is a subtle and difficult art. But all manner of grief and disruption can be avoided when a leader graciously acknowledges that it is time for somebody else to step in.

Pace yourself

Above all, the leader of a start-up has to display a fine sense of timing. Yes, you want to move fast initially. Speed kills, as they say. There can be such a thing as 'first mover advantage'.

But businesses that last know when to be bold, and when to consolidate. They take judicious risks. Start-ups can burn out if that sense of pace and timing isn't right. So this is the last item on the desired list of qualities in the leader of a start-up: the ability to judge when to step on the gas and when to change down a gear or two. Your colleagues will thank you for that kind of sensitive leadership, and perform better because of it.

The prize for getting all this right can be great. What is it that Mick Jagger and the boys like to sing? 'If you start me up I'll never stop, never, never stop . . .'

SMEs

Small and medium-sized enterprises are where the action is. This is the 'real economy'. These are the service providers, the contractors, the people who do the work that the big boys (initially) get paid for. They are the lifeblood of outsourcing, and often the heartbeat of local communities. Their shares are very rarely traded on stock markets. They are in private, or family, ownership. Top salaries are not on another planet when compared with the rest of the workforce. This is real business, and it calls for real leadership.

Perhaps this is why such a revered management guru as Tom Peters is a fan of SMEs. First as a consultant at McKinsey, and then as a sought-after speaker and author, Peters has spent a lot time with mega corporations and grand C-suite figures around the world. But now, as he told the Corporate Rebels website, he usually finds stimulation and creativity elsewhere.

'Who cares what the big enterprises are doing?' he said. 'They are boring! Just study, visit and write about small and medium-sized businesses. The really interesting stuff is happening there.'[53]

What is it that makes SMEs special? And what does this mean for those who seek to lead them? They are special because they are still operating on a human scale. They are close to their customers. They haven't forgotten what got them into business in the first place. They haven't acquired lots of other businesses or sprouted all sorts of subsidiaries all over the place.

For leaders, this represents an advantage but also imposes a discipline. The staff will expect you to know everybody's name, and a few details about each of them. They will expect to see you on site. And they will also expect you to understand the nitty gritty of what their jobs entail.

This all serves as a good reminder of what basic leadership and management are about: paying attention, listening to people and displaying basic competence. The SME is also a warning and a rebuke about growth for its own sake, the 'undisciplined pursuit of more' as the guru Jim Collins has characterized it. Companies, especially those whose share are not traded, could instead concentrate on getting 'better, not bigger', as the management writer Charles Handy has always argued. Does the London Symphony Orchestra want to have 20 per cent more violinists next year? Or does it just want to hone the quality of its performances? Are the owners of Château Pétrus planting lots of new vines or are they just trying to make great wine (and, by the way, keep the price of their product up by managing the supply)? SMEs, the good ones at least, are keeping it real.

Transitions and life cycles

When a start-up has made it past its first few difficult months and years it is no longer a start-up: it has wings, and should be able to fly. This is the first major life-cycle transition which leadership has to make. And not every leader can do this. A founder entrepreneur may be the right person to prove a business concept and get through the early days. But once the business is established and needs to focus on finding new customers and markets perhaps a different sort of leader will be required.

Recognizing this takes maturity on the part of the founder, or perhaps a firmness of touch from early investors. It is not a mark of failure to move aside, merely a sign that the former start-up needs a new approach at the top. Many entrepreneurs want to move on at this point in any case, to go and develop new ideas and fight new battles.

The leader of a growing SME has to convey this need for change to staff too. Where once there was an element of experimentation, even play, about launching a new business, the growing (and maturing) business needs some new disciplines. Order books will with any luck be growing, and supply chain relationships may be getting deeper and more complicated. IT requirements may grow too.

But other disciplines that got you through the start-up phase have to be maintained. Cash is still king. 'Payables' (fees owed) have to be realized. Costs should not be allowed to spiral.

And some of the other tell-tale signs of thoughtless growth have to be kept at bay. You don't necessarily need more meetings. You don't necessarily need to introduce lots of formal procedures. Yes, the numbers involved in running the business are getting bigger, but that doesn't mean you have to acquire the bureaucracy and stifling formality found in larger firms and which, in all likelihood, drove some of your colleagues to work in a smaller business in the first place.

Golden opportunity

Leadership is not about acquiring bigger and brasher office space, larger company cars and ever more luxurious hotel accommodation. It is not about 'scaling up' with no greater purpose other than getting bigger. It's about helping teams of people to give of their best, reminding busy colleagues about what really matters, making sure that the main thing remains the main thing, as seven habits guru Stephen Covey used to say.

The encouraging growth in independent bookshops and craft beer companies, along with the survival of the best local restaurants, bars and specialist shops, tells us that customers value the personal touch that only SMEs can provide. A loyal, steady flow of customers is something you can build a lasting business on.

The brilliant guys at Regent Sounds in London's Denmark Street, who have already sold my older daughter two guitars and will probably succeed in selling her more, are the perfect example of this. (And for repairs you just take the 'Stairway to Kevin' next door. Really.)

Small is beautiful, German economist EF Schumacher said. He had a point. It is often overlooked, still. His philosophy doesn't just make for a better business, but it might just help save the planet, too.

Public (listed) company

Chief executive is nice-sounding job title to have, but if you are the boss of a public (that is, stock-market listed) company the label itself provides no added protection at all. If anything, it can hang a target around your neck. The buck stops with the CEO, who is supposed to be leading the work which delivers results to keep investors happy. If the market does not like what it is hearing your share price will be marked down, financial analysts will be harsh and your business will be more vulnerable to take over. A public company whose shares trade freely is always for sale. If a buyer has enough cash and desire you will be bought out, unless shareholders resist.

Why do people still aspire to add the initials 'CEO' to their CV? Power is attractive, and being a CEO might, from the outside, look like a powerful job. It still is, of course, but perhaps not quite to the same extent that it once was.

Corporate governance reforms have changed some of the rules of the game. Dictators are no longer meant to be allowed to get away with dictating. Non-executive directors are supposed to bring independent thought and 'challenge' to the boardroom. Big decisions should be taken collectively, by boards and senior management teams, and not just at the whim of one person.

So much for theory. In practice, dominant CEOs can still get away with a lot, especially in a rising market or when the financial performance looks good. The classic life cycle of a CEO – inherit a mess, look good for a bit, stay too long, get kicked out, new CEO inherits the mess – is still more or less in place.

Better CEOs

The allure of power draws in ambitious types who want to get to the top. Financial rewards for CEOs can be vast, and have increased enormously over the past thirty years. The rise in top pay coincided with the collapse of the Soviet system and the 'triumph' of free market capitalism. These parallel trends are perhaps not unrelated.

The linking of CEO pay to share prices has driven this

trend. This was originally done with a good and honest intention: to align the interests of senior management with the shareholders. But, as the saying goes, what gets measured gets manipulated. CEOs now have an incentive – a perverse one – to get the share price up quickly (and they know they might be out of a job soon) by starving the business of investment and using spare capital to buy back shares rather than spending those funds more creatively. Shareholders have been complicit in this. A win-win then? Hardly. Public companies have become financial engineering machines rather than innovative or productive powerhouses, with the consequences we have seen for ordinary workers' wages and general productivity. This has had political consequences too: Brexit, and Trump.

Good CEOs of public companies do keep shareholders happy – they have to – but not at the expense of the long term. They recognize the illusory nature of short term reporting. Paul Polman, CEO of Unilever between 2009 and 2018, announced pretty soon on taking up the job that he would no longer be providing so-called 'quarterly guidance' – figures – on how the company was doing. He did not see such data as meaningful. Jeff Bezos, founder and CEO of Amazon, has a similar view. Although the company does provide quarterly data, Bezos has not bothered taking part in an earnings call with analysts for a decade. He believes that the next thirteen weeks' figures are already decided, and so are the next thirteen weeks after that, and the thirteen weeks after that. The decisions he and his team are taking today will bear fruit (or not) only years from now. (You will be able to read more about Polman and Bezos in chapter 7.)

Who are these guys? (They are mostly guys)

The *Financial Times'* Rana Foroohar reported on her impression of CEO behaviour after attending the World Economic Forum in Davos. 'CEOs talk a good game about changing culture, but business still rewards mainly the most extreme personalities,' she wrote.

> Davos is always a good reminder of how being a CEO is like being a competitive athlete, or even a gladiator. These people get up at 6am, go to bed at 1am, work out like crazy, don't eat much (one head of a European financial firm in Davos was on a diet of only apples), never see their families and often have anger issues. Why wouldn't they, when they are scheduled in 15-minute increments six days a week, under 24-7 pressure, and have a shelf life of three years? [54]

This is all very macho. (In the next chapter we will consider the issues which lie behind this state of affairs.) But the problem is clear. If we want better public companies then we need better people becoming CEOs of them. And that means doing something about the supply chain of future CEOs.

It also means reinstating the dignity and purpose of the public company as a virtuous and worthwhile corporate structure. The number of public companies has shrunk quite dramatically over the past twenty years – by a half in the US and a similar figure in the UK. But we need public companies to employ people, to invest, to pay dividends to pension funds and to be transparent and so help to raise standards. Not all private sector 'wealth creation' should take place in the dark. Good CEOs embrace the daylight as a discipline and as a way of spurring better performance.

After her Davos visit, the *FT*'s Foroohar was uncertain how this could all be achieved. 'Frankly, I don't know what the solution to this problem is,' she wrote. 'But I do know that we can talk all we want about "cognitive diversity", and kinder corporate cultures, but until we can create a different way to be a global leader, not much will change. By the way, this is an under-explored reason behind women not taking on more multinational CEO jobs; many think they are dreadful and don't want them.'

In fact, we probably know how we want CEOs to behave: we want them to lead a strong top team, take judicious risks, reward people fairly, provide work, goods and services, and to make a profit sustainably.

Simple to describe, but not easy to do.

Public sector/not-for-profit

The bottom line is the bottom line. If you are a 'for-profit' business – a private enterprise – you face some hard financial realities which cannot be avoided. There will be competition for market share. If you don't have enough paying customers you will lose money, your costs will be higher than your revenue and eventually you will go bust. It's harsh at times but it's also pretty straightforward. If you don't offer what people want you will be out of business quite soon.

In the public and so-called 'not-for-profit' sectors (we will come back to that unappealing label), things are rather more complicated. The 'profit motive' does not exist. You are there not to provide people with things that they want, necessarily, but with things that they need.

Competition for market share does not really exist in the same way, because there is not – or perhaps should not be – a market as such to compete in. The public sector provides public goods – healthcare, education, social services, policing – and is concerned with offering a service, not simply with making money. It is a different kind of task altogether.

[We should also mention those businesses such as social enterprises, mutual organizations and some partnerships which strictly (and fiscally) speaking are also 'not-for-profit', although both inside and outside look and feel pretty much like a commercial operation. However, these are not really the subject of this chapter.]

Mission and purpose

The great advantage public sector leaders enjoy, in principle, is that there is no need to create a pretentious, bamboozling 'mission statement' in the way that private sector businesses seem to feel obliged to – perhaps because, in truth, they often lack true purpose. No, the public sector is providing essential services, and it takes remarkably poor leadership (which does exist I'm afraid) to confuse or mislead public sector workers to such an extent that they don't understand what it is they are supposed to be doing.

The management guru Peter Drucker once suggested that we should manage people as if they were volunteers – meaning that the profit motive (and the desire to get paid) alone cannot inspire greater commitment. But public sector leaders do not need (indeed are unable) to dangle large financial incentives in front of their staff.

The commitment of the public sector worker should

never be taken for granted. In an age of austerity and wage freezes this is exactly what has happened. It is a crying shame. Finite resources in the public sector always call for greater resourcefulness. (In the famous phrase usually attributed to the Nobel prize-winning scientist Ernest Rutherford: 'We've got no money so we have got to think.'[55]) But leading at a time of persistent cuts is no easy task. And where cuts and reorganizations lead only to cynicism and greater inefficiency, the very notion of leadership has been turned on its head.

Inspiring commitment

The 'not-for-profit' label is another downer of a phrase – there should be a prize for someone who can come up with something better. Just as 'non-executive directors' can sound like an enfeebled version of the real thing, so not-for-profit can sound like something less valuable than for-profit. And yet it is really only a distinction that is made for tax and legal purposes. It should not be seen to imply that there is something less valuable about the work being carried out. Who wants to have a job title or work in a sector that starts with a negative?

But great public sector leaders can do remarkable things. Think of a headteacher who helps to revive a once failing school. With high expectations for both pupils and staff a good head can transform lives. Think of a competent chief executive of a large general hospital trust. The complexity involved in leading such an organization is immense. Mistakes can become great scandals. Lives are lost. And yet the teamwork ensured by good leadership in a hospital can work wonders, even in a world of limited – that is to say rationed – resources. Equally, a good (and not overpaid) university vice chancellor can ensure their institution is serving society through its teaching, scholarship and entrepreneurialism. The profit motive has little to do with any of these kind of success stories. There is competition, but it is competition for reputation and esteem. It is non-financial. And arguably so much the better for that.

Public leadership

The idea of leadership has been besmirched through the greed, stupidity and corruption of some prominent executives. Corrupt and dishonest political leaders do harm as well.

And yet good public leadership can have precisely the opposite effect. Good public leaders have a ready answer to Jim Collins' important question referred to in the introduction to this book: 'what are you in it for?' They are not in it for the money or themselves. They are there to serve others while providing a lead and a sense of direction.

Dan Cable, Professor of Organizational Behaviour at London Business School, describes this sort of leadership well in his book *Alive at Work*. When these sorts of leaders are present, he says, 'Work is managed by servant leaders, who help shape the vision, and then try to learn from employees and help them accomplish their goals rather than emphasising hierarchy. When leaders express feelings of uncertainty and humility, they end up encouraging a learning mindset in others, which increases experimentation and innovation.'[56]

In this way, the public sector can be every bit as dynamic, innovative and resourceful as any private sector organization. What is more, there can be a big commercial upside to doing good public work. As Peter Drucker also pointed out, every social problem is in fact a business opportunity in disguise.

And one other thing: the public sector creates wealth, too. Never let it be said otherwise. The schools and colleges which provide education, the health service which gets people well and back to work: these are forces for good which help to support a successful economy. Good public leadership has been private for too long. We need to see more of it in every sense.

5:

LET'S TALK ABOUT SEX

Are women leaders different?

The best boss I ever had and the worst boss I ever had were women. (Not the same one, incidentally.) What does this prove? Nothing at all. But in a chapter which is inevitably going to involve a certain degree of generalization it is worth issuing this health warning in advance. Not all men, women, people are the same. However, we do need to talk about male and female leaders, and ask both where the differences lie and how a better understanding of these differences might benefit us all.

It is the right time to have this debate. In fact, it is massively overdue. While social change and attitudes have progressed, slowly, over the past five decades or so, many workplaces seem to have resisted even this gradual pace of development. The upper echelons of businesses and organizations do not look so very different from the way they looked many years ago. Arguably, there has been more change in terms of the social or class background of bosses than there has been in terms of gender.

We will consider some of the reasons why this is so in the following pages. But first it is worth asking: are women leaders different? And what, by implication, are businesses missing out on by not promoting and encouraging more women to take up senior positions?

How women lead

In an influential article for the *McKinsey Quarterly* in 2008 ('Centred leadership: how talented women thrive'), Joanna Barsh, Susie Cranston and Rebecca Craske drew on extensive research to describe the ways in which successful women lead, and showed how this might differ from traditional male models of behaviour.[57]

They found that there are five main elements to a style of leadership they called 'centred'. This is not a synonym for 'female'. However, it is a leadership model which they found involved women predominantly and overwhelmingly. (It's not that men can't do it. It's just that they found many fewer who did.)

The first key element of centred leadership is meaning, or 'finding your strengths and putting them to work in the service of an inspiring purpose', as the authors put it.

The second is managing energy, or 'knowing where your energy comes from, where it goes, and what you can do to manage it'. This is particularly important owing to the different (and much larger) emotional demands that are made on women because of caring responsibilities at home.

A third aspect is positive framing, or 'adopting a more constructive way to view your world, expand your horizons, and gain the resilience to move ahead even when bad things happen'. Women at work may enjoy fewer support networks – there may just be fewer supportive people (women) on hand – and may also be handed 'glass cliff' assignments which no man is brave enough to take on. So resilience of this kind is essential.

A fourth and related part of centred leadership is connecting, or 'identifying who can help you grow, building stronger relationships, and increasing your sense of belonging'. Women may sometimes find mentors at work but they often lack sponsors – people (not necessarily always men) who will speak up for you when you are not there. So making these connections is crucial. Lastly, centred leaders are good at engaging, or 'finding your voice, becoming self-reliant and confident by accepting opportunities and the inherent risks they bring, and collaborating with others'.

Without falling into the trap of believing that women simply 'do feelings' better than men – we have surely all worked with women for whom this is not the case – the McKinsey authors do highlight the need for emotional intelligence and awareness.

> Centred leadership emphasises the role of positive emotions. A few characteristics particularly distinguish women from their male counterparts in the workplace. First, women can more often opt out of it than men can. Second, their double burden – motherhood and management – drains energy in a particularly challenging way. Third, they tend to experience emotional ups and downs more often and more intensely than most men do.'

Centred leadership is not an option reserved for women. But they do seem to have a head start when it comes to trying to adopt it. So in some ways the answer for men who want to become better leaders is ... be more like women.

Testosterone Rex . . . or doesn't

Aha, you say, it is no use fighting nature. That devilish hormone testosterone, generally found in larger quantities in men than in women, drives male behaviour. There's a reason why the trading floors of financial institutions are dominated by risk-taking men: all that testosterone encourages them to be braver and even reckless – it's known as the 'risky shift'. If Lehman Brothers had been called Lehman Sisters, so the old quip goes, maybe the financial crisis could have been avoided.

Well, yes and no. But mainly no. Sex is not destiny, and even testosterone, as the psychologist and author Cordelia Fine has shown[58], does not determine everything. Societal structures, cultural norms and learned behavioural responses all have their part to play.

The more humdrum but important truth is that there are certain female leadership characteristics or traits that men would do well to emulate. Women seem, in general, not to expect (rarely 'demand') such vast, overblown salaries – this is certainly the case in the FTSE100 index, where of course only five or six female CEOs are to be found, all of them in the bottom quartile for pay packages. You may that this is a bad thing, and that true equality would mean equally massive pay for women bosses. And yet women bosses in general do not seem to feel the need to declare of their pay package 'mine's bigger than yours'. They seem, in general, to share the old-fashioned idea that leaders should be putting more in than they take out. This too is a point of differentiation with male bosses.

So how else should male leaders try and behave differently? We shall consider this question next.

What men need to do

Let's be blunt: if there's one thing holding women back at work, it's men. Yes of course it is a bit more complicated than that in practice. Some women choose not to compete with the self-appointed 'alpha males'. Some genuinely have other priorities. Others may leave to start their own businesses. But it is also true that, although at graduate/entry level top employers are hiring women for at least 50 per cent of new positions, and often rather more, a decade later already the numbers have slipped a bit, and by the time senior appointments are being made most of the top jobs are going to men.

This represents a massive loss of potential and productive output. It makes no sense. And yet it continues. Inertia remains a powerful negative force. The chaps at the top may talk about making changes, they may even believe that they are sincere about doing so. But action is lacking. What do men in positions of authority need to do to make it possible for women to get to the top in equal (or at least much larger) numbers? Here are a few ideas:

Question your assumptions

Part of the difficulty for men of a certain generation, who have reached the top doing things their way, is that they simply may not recognize the need for change. And even if they do, they may not know how to bring change about. Senior men need to wake up and realize the extent of their problems. They are losing thousands of talented people every year. The environment they are creating at work is inhospitable to too many talented women.

Men may look around the top table and feel that everything is ok. There may never have been many women at the top, and yet the business seems to be doing fine. Why change now?

The reason is that other, new businesses will emerge that grasp the opportunities better. They will attract more than their fair share of young female talent. They will create more vibrant, creative, productive workplaces. And pretty soon things won't be fine at all.

Consider doing things differently

Businesses have talked the talk on flexibility for over two decades. The PR advisers have drafted the nice speeches, and the HR department has written sensible policies. But what has changed? Not nearly enough. (The newly released data on gender pay gaps confirm that there are just lots more men than women in the more senior – and higher paid – roles. We shall say a bit more about this in the following pages.)

So leaders need to make a public commitment to flexibility. They need to be seen to be practising it themselves. They need to promote men and women who work flexibly. They should make it clear that parents – mothers and fathers – can get on at the business even if they take extended breaks. Good employers want their best people to return to work after having children if that is what they want to do, suffering no career penalty for having interrupted their time in the office. It's way beyond time that this became a real, meaningful option for many more people at work.

Actively sponsor women

As well as flexibility, (male) bosses need to move beyond mere (sometimes patronizing) mentoring to full-scale sponsorship. As there have not been many women at the top in the past, aspiring women will need vocal and visible champions. Who will speak up for future women leaders if they are not already in the key meetings where things get decided? Are women getting plum, stretch assignments or being given important divisions to run? Do the senior men mean what they say and act on it? Or have women already smelt a rat and are looking to leave? Without effective sponsorship of talented women nothing will change for the better.

Embrace quotas

A symbol of meaningful change is the introduction of quotas. These are not popular with everybody. The threat of quotas, raised by Lord (Mervyn) Davies in his work on boardroom diversity, did make a difference in the UK. From a very low baseline the number of non-executive directors rose quite fast to around the 25 per cent mark. Not good enough, but progress nonetheless.[59]

Of course, some worry that quotas could lead to tokenism, or the promotion of second-rate people over the heads of others. Others argue that the idea is simply patronizing. Anyone would want to feel that a promotion has been made on merit. All these risks must be guarded against.

But I think the former EU Commissioner Viviane Reding got it right when she said she doesn't like quotas, but she likes 'the results they bring.'[60] Some change has to be forced through, especially when the men in power are reluctant to do things differently. If men won't promote and support women, legislators will have to make it happen for them.*

Shut the f*** up and listen

Lastly, the 'mansplaining', and the constant interrupting of women has to stop. We need an end to that familiar tendency joked about bitterly in these terms – 'That's a great idea Susan. Now, perhaps one of the men would like to suggest it?'

Any good leader ought to be able to listen. But what the dreadfully slow rate of progress reveals is that male bosses have not been listening to female colleagues over the years. They have not heard what they were being told. And even if they have heard, they have not acted on it, which amounts to the same thing.

This will go against the grain for some male bosses, who like to speak in long paragraphs which demonstrate what a profound and special grasp they have of the mega-trends and also the subtleties which have passed everybody else by. But if they listen they might learn something, and learn to do better.

These are all measures that the men in power have to take if they want their best women to stay and make a career with them. We need more women leaders if we want to have better leadership. And for some men, I regret to say, time's up.

---

* For more on quotas see: Pryce V. (2015). *Why Women Need Quotas*, Biteback Publishing, London, UK

Gender-balanced leadership and organizations

It's almost fifty years since the UK's Equal Pay Act of 1970 was made law. It has been illegal since that time for men and women doing the same job to get paid at different rates. In 2018, new gender pay gap disclosure rules required larger UK employers to produce data on what men and women at work are being paid, and how large the gaps on average are. Gender pay gaps are not a sign that the Equal Pay Act is being flouted. But they do reveal the structural imbalances – and injustices, and inefficiencies – which still afflict many organizations. Businesses that remain very top heavy (in terms of having many more men in senior roles) have larger gender pay gaps.

Also in 2018, the UK's Equalities and Human Rights Commission published a large report ('Turning the tables: ending sexual harassment at work'), which argued that not nearly enough had been done to tackle ongoing sexual harassment at work, and that indeed such behaviour was in danger of being 'normalized'.[61]

The commission's chief executive, Rebecca Hilsenrath, said:

> We set out to discover how sexual harassment at work is dealt with by employers and how it is experienced by individuals. What we found was truly shocking. There is a lack of consistent, effective action being taken by employers, and people's careers and mental and physical health have been damaged as a result.
>
> Corrosive cultures have silenced individuals and sexual harassment has been normalised. We underesti-

mate the extent and we are complacent as to impact. We need urgent action to turn the tables in British workplaces; shifting from the current culture of people risking their jobs and health in order to report harassment, to placing the onus on employers to prevent and resolve it.

This all makes for depressing reading. And it points to a grand failure of leadership. We are still so far from establishing healthy, safe working cultures where people are rewarded and treated fairly. Better, 'gender-balanced leadership' would help eradicate some of these problems. What is it and how can we achieve it?

Gender-balanced leadership

This is a term coined by Avivah Wittenberg-Cox, a writer and consultant. In a series of books and articles over the past decade, Wittenberg-Cox has made a practical and highly business-friendly case for a better balance between the sexes at work.

In an article for the *Harvard Business Review* in November 2016 titled 'How CEOs can put gender balance on the agenda at their companies', she set out in clear terms what gender balance could be like and how to achieve it.

Many CEOs insist that they are 'gender blind'. But here's where I argue that it's time to become 'gender bilingual' instead. That doesn't mean we speak two different languages. It means we deeply understand different cultures and build bridges between them to include everyone. It also means replacing women's networks and other women-branded initiatives with inclusive approaches that unite men and women rather than separating them. [62]

Wittenberg-Cox neatly summarizes why true gender balance has proved elusive so far:

Too many companies are wasting time and money recruiting more women when the real issue is that they aren't retaining or promoting them. Men typically experience the 'Peter Principle', meaning they are promoted to their level of incompetence, whereas women often experience the 'Paula Principle', meaning they are under-promoted across the board. This is creating situations where many multinationals are skewing female at the bottom without ever affecting the balance at the top, to their great frustration.

Wittenberg-Cox warns against tokenism. 'Getting one woman from a support function onto your team and then asking her to lead a gender initiative is doomed to fail,' she wrote. 'Recognize that the people you will most need to convince are today's dominant majority. It's better to have any efforts be visibly led by one of them.'

And, contrary to the view I offered earlier, Wittenberg-Cox suggests crude quotas should be avoided:

Always insist on meritocracy. Avoid announcing a goal of 'having the leadership team be 30 per cent women by 2020', a type of pronouncement that is still an all-too-common irritant in many companies. I suggest that if you never say the word 'women' again, you will save yourself a lot of grief. Talk about 'talent' or 'customers' or 'balance' – words that avoid alienation as you strategically create a more representative balance for tomorrow.

This is perhaps an idealistic view. People at work – men and women – will know what you are talking about with terms such as 'balance'. But the warning on crude percentages is a good one.

Above all Wittenberg-Cox argues that change must be led visibly from the top, and with sincere commitment.

> In most companies today, managers are still more willing to accept women taking parental leave than men. Until this evens out, gender balance will remain out of reach. If you want women to be leaders, encourage men to be fathers . . . You will need to get all your managers to buy in to the benefits of balance, and then become skilled at selling it to others. Their readiness to do either will depend on what you as the CEO say and do. Successful gender balance starts – or fails – at the top.

What next?

Feminism, in all of its waves and manifestations, has achieved a great deal. And yet fairness and equality of opportunity at work still seem a long way off. It will take another fifty years, at the current rate of progress, to reach true pay parity – one hundred years after a law was passed to bring that about.

Better leaders of the future, male and female, will put some of these lingering injustices behind us. Let's take a brief look at what this more positive future might be like.

Future leaders, men and women

So much for the criticism and the description of what is wrong. What sort of more positive future could we build if male and female leaders could work better together? Here are a few thoughts.

Collaborative

If the imbalance between the sexes was finally brought to an end – at work as well as at home – what sort of benefits would we see? If a greater sense of justice prevailed the barriers to more creative and collaborative work would come down. Workplaces might attain that quality sometimes found in Scandinavian firms, where genuinely flexible working – including shared parental leave – is more common. An atmosphere of mutual respect would allow for more diversity of thought and behaviour. Productivity, creativity and innovation would all increase.

Complementary

This healthier workplace culture would arise from the recognition that men and women are not the same, clearly, but they are complementary. The customer base is made up of men and women – although the large majority of domestic purchasing decisions are still taken by women – and so a workforce which does not contain men and women, with each able to contribute, is unbalanced. If men and women at work are both seen to be able to rise up the hierarchy there will be greater encouragement for all to give of their best.

Equal opportunities

But for this to happen the dream of equal opportunities has to become a reality. This is about will, not business cycles or fashion. Women have been very patient, probably too patient, waiting for fairness. It is yet to arrive. Hence the controversial discussion over quotas – a flawed instrument, perhaps, but also an effective and probably necessary one, given the delays and foot-dragging we have seen. We will never see more women leaders in their rightful place at the head of businesses and organizations without truly equal opportunities.

Family-friendly

Another nice bit of corporate speak which needs to be made real is the talk of flexibility and being a 'family-friendly' employer. Dr Maja Korica of Warwick Business School summed up the situation well in a speech given at Westminster in 2018:

'As it stands [in the UK], parents can share up to fifty weeks of leave and thirty-seven weeks of statutory pay after birth of a child. Fathers can also take two weeks of paternity leave, under certain conditions. Here's the rub though: employers are only obliged to pay them £140.98 per week, or 90 per cent of earnings if that is lower, unless additional provisions are made. The UK government estimates that only 2 per cent of eligible parents currently take shared parental leave. In comparison, in Sweden in 2016, 27 per cent of all parental leave benefits were paid to men, up from 12 per cent in 1999. Research shows that old-fashioned gender expectations mean men who take parental leave in such an environment face social penalties for doing so. Focusing on flexible working and shared parental leave would address such biases too, again resulting in better outcomes and productivity for all, not to mention lives and societies.[63]

Sustainable

Better, gender-balanced leadership will help build more successful, more sustainable organizations. That is what this is all about. It is not a question of doing the 'politically correct' thing. It is about building and sustaining businesses that work. We cannot keep shutting out or losing up to 50 per cent of the talent in the workforce. Good leadership – real leadership – would make this an absolute priority, and would put demanding targets in place to make sure that substantial progress is made, quickly.

6:

THE LANGUAGE OF LEADERS

Purpose

'Having lost sight of our objectives, we redoubled our efforts' runs an old gag, written by the American cartoonist Walt Kelly. It makes a good, timeless point. Work should have a purpose. Part of the job of leaders is to let people know what that purpose is. This is more important than it used to be. In more deferential times, status and rank alone could command a degree of compliance, however grudging. Now people are more likely to ask 'why?' when required to do something. Leaders should be ready with an answer. 'To what end?' is another way of asking the same thing. If people at work share and understand a purpose there is less likelihood of the question ever being asked.

Big claims are made for the power or purpose – perhaps a bit too big at times. The Big Innovation Centre published a report in 2017 which claimed UK businesses alone could be worth £130 billion more if they were better 'organized around clear corporate purposes that unite all stakeholders'.[64] That's a lot of money. Perhaps it's true.

There is evidence to support the idea that weak or badly expressed purpose is costly. In a survey of 1,000 employees by a consultancy called Kin&Co, 42 per cent said their company does not act according to its expressed purpose and values, and 53 per cent said their company's marketing does not reflect the reality of what they do. This gap between espoused purpose and reality made 49 per cent of them want to leave the business, and 68 per cent said this gap would have a bad impact on their work, reducing their productivity and making them lose trust in their leaders. At the same time, 72 per cent said they'd be more likely to stay at their company if they were more emotionally connected to their work.[65] This is what a clear purpose can do for you.

Big bucks

As Rob Goffee, Gareth Jones and Roger Steare pointed out in an essay for *Management Today*, the talk of purpose is rising up the corporate agenda and in the heart of the world of institutional investment as well.[66]

One of the biggest beasts of this investment world is Larry Fink, chairman and CEO of BlackRock, which manages almost $6 trillion in assets. Mr Fink writes a letter to the CEOs of the businesses it invests in every year. His 2018 letter focused on purpose and governance. He wrote that 'companies must benefit all of their stakeholders, including shareholders, employees, customers, and the communities in which they operate'.

And he added:

Without a sense of purpose, no company, either public or private, can achieve its full potential. It will ultimately lose the licence to operate from key stakeholders. It will succumb to short-term pressures to distribute earnings, and, in the process, sacrifice investments in employee development, innovation, and capital expenditures that are necessary for long-term growth. [67]

A report from the Korn Ferry Institute from 2016 showed that consumer sector companies with an authentic focus on purpose achieved compounded annual growth rates of 9.85 per cent compared with 2.4 per cent for the whole Standard & Poor consumer sector.[68]

Goffee, Jones and Steare also cited recent research by Amy Wrzesniewski, Clark McCauley, Paul Rozen and Barry Schwartz, which has shown that people tend to be motivated by one of three purposes, which they describe as:

1. Work as a vehicle for material reward, but not fulfilling in and of itself

2. Work as a means toward social status, achievement, and prestige

3. Work inherently meaningful and rich in purpose[69]

But it is only among those in the third group, Goffee, Jones and Steare say, that greater personal and professional satisfaction is found, and that this also correlates strongly with greater success and higher performance.

Codifying purpose

The British charity Blueprint for Better Business has spent several years trying to spread the message about purpose through boardrooms and offices. It makes a clear and cogent case on its website for the uses of purpose, explaining:

A business needs to make a profit otherwise it cannot survive – but making a profit is not the purpose of business. There needs to be a connection between the purpose of the business, the benefit to society and to all the other stakeholders: employees want a job, customers want the right goods or services at the right price, suppliers want to be treated properly, investors want a return . . . purpose is the glue that brings it all together and creates long term sustainable performance. [70]

A corporate purpose has four main elements or reasons for existing, they say:

1. To inspire people to contribute their personal energy to a collective venture

2. To reveal the human face of what the organization is working to achieve

3. To ensure an authentic connection between what the organization believes, what it says, what it means and what it does

4. To enable people to make practical choices about what they do day to day, using the purpose as a constant reference point

And a good purpose has three main qualities. It should be inspiring, authentic and practical. It will be inspiring if it speaks to the people who are the intended beneficiaries of the purpose. It will be authentic if the purpose underpins business decisions rather than just being a communications exercise. The company's goods and services should embody this purpose. And it will be practical if is clear enough so that positive choices can be made. Can it be used to review what services and products should be provided? Can it be used to encourage and reward good behaviour?

The purpose of purpose

As so often, John Kay has summed up the use and role of corporate purpose best:

> We must breathe to live but breathing is not the purpose of life. The purpose of a corporation is to produce goods and services to meet economic and social needs, to create satisfying and rewarding employment, to earn returns for its shareholders and other investors, and to make a positive contribution to the social and physical environment in which it operates.[71]

And in terms of putting this into effect, the American writer Daniel Coyle gives us a good hint in in his book *The Culture Code – The Secret of Highly Successful Groups*. He says: 'Purpose isn't about tapping into some mystical internal drive but rather about creating simple beacons that focus attention and engagement on the shared goal. Successful cultures do this by relentlessly seeking ways to tell and retell their story.' [72]

If you haven't got a purpose in your business or personal life it would be a good idea to try and get one as soon as you can. It will certainly help you to be a better leader.

Values

Rule books may be necessary, but they can get in the way of what you want to do. The bulkier they are, the more packed with rules, the less dynamic your organization will be. How much better if the people you work with share certain values and a similar approach to the tasks in hand.

Good leaders will talk quite a lot about values. It helps them convey what sort of behaviour they hope to see from their people. But talk will only get you so far. Leaders themselves need to set an example and model the sort of behaviour they want. And their decisions should embody their espoused values too. When company leadership says one thing but acts in way that undermines faith in what they are saying, cynicism builds and engagement is destroyed.

The risk of talking a good talk on values, but failing to live up those high standards, has been well described by the Nobel prize-wining economist Joseph Stiglitz. Having watched the world's elite at Davos in 2018, Professor Stiglitz wrote disdainfully about what he had witnessed first hand in a blog post:.

> CEOs from around the world begin most of their speeches by affirming the importance of values. Their activities, they proclaim, are aimed not just at maximising profits for shareholders, but also at creating a better future for their workers, the communities in which they work, and the world more generally. They may even pay lip service to the risks posed by climate change and inequality.
>
> But, by the end of their speeches this year, any remaining illusion about the values motivating Davos CEOs was shattered. The risk that these CEOs seemed most concerned about is the populist backlash against the kind of globalisation that they have shaped – and from which they have benefited immensely. [73]

Values that work

Good values can support an approach to business that is sometimes described as 'enlightened self-interest'. Behaving well can be profitable. Harvard Business School's Michael Porter, with his colleague Mark Kramer, developed the idea of 'creating shared value', an advance, commercially, on conventional 'corporate social responsibility' thinking.[74]

Another HBS professor, the ethnographer Ryan Raffaelli, has been studying the remarkable survival and indeed flourishing of independent bookshops in the US in the age of Amazon. Three C words – don't worry, clean ones – lie at the heart of this success. He has found that by establishing a sense of community, curating a friendly environment and convening support and interest these bookshops have kept their businesses alive.

'What we're learning is that values can drive growth and engagement in ways that can trump what we often think about as economic viability,' Professor Raffaelli told the LitHub website.

Independent bookshops are of course being menaced by the speed, muscle and distribution power of Amazon. And yet they still hold an attraction for their most loyal customers.

So indies decided, we can't let go of this community. And that is a separate consideration from questions like 'should we try to have sales?' and 'do we have to worry about how many titles do we need in the store to compete?'

When you have a clean idea about a higher order value system that also is aligned with a consumer value system, it becomes less about the product and more about those values that attach the two together.

Independent booksellers realized and were clear about, 'this is what we have to hold onto and this what we have to let go of'. And those decisions were based on values.

For a lot of organizations, when they're making those decisions after facing sort of a technological shock, those choices often aren't values based. And I think for the indies, they were principled. [75]

So values are the answer to everything? Not so fast. As the philosopher Baroness Onora O'Neill points out in a chapter of Routledge's *Companion to Human Rights*, the word has now been adopted so widely, especially in workplaces, that confusion could be the result. She writes:

This issue [of moral choices] is often obscured by the promiscuous use of the term 'value' to characterise whatever individuals happen to choose or prefer, which leaves it fatally obscure whether empirical or normative claims are at stake. Where empirical claims are made about individuals' choices or preferences, there will be no general reason to see anything (let alone everything) that is chosen or preferred by agents as valuable: much that is chosen or preferred may be worthless or bad . . . Referring to whatever individuals choose as 'values' confuses empirical claims about preferences with normative claims about what is valuable, thereby conflating subjective and ethical claims . . . If individuals can choose, define and redefine 'values' and 'identities', ethical claims are replaced by subjective claims. [76]

Which is a careful and scholarly way of describing what we see so often around us in business: people behaving badly even as they claim to be driven and supported by great values. When the Cambridge Analytica/Facebook scandal erupted after the EU referendum, the former CEO Alexander Nix was suspended, and the company declared that 'in the view of the board, Mr Nix's recent comments secretly recorded by Channel4 News do not represent the values or operations of the firm.' And yet Mr Nix had been captured describing enthusiastically precisely what the company had been getting up to.

Values assuredly do matter. They can't always be set down formally in rule books. They are embodied in people's behaviour and the choices that they make. Leader are right to talk about them. But better still, they should act in the way they want others too. Actions speak louder than words. And when it comes to corporate values, leaders' actions speak loudest of all.

Strategy

If there is one thing that people will look to the leader for, it's strategy. This is the legacy of history, and indeed ancient language. *Strategos* is a Greek word meaning a general in the army. Strategic ideas are supposed to be Big and Important and come straight from the general's tent.

This heavy legacy has endured in business. Strategy just sounds rather cool, doesn't it? It is, to deploy that already over-used and under-justified adjective, 'sexy'. But it also a term that is misused, and which misleads. The business writer and academic John Kay pointed this out several years ago. The word strategy, he said, should in fact be seen as a synonym for 'expensive'. Hence when a firm describes itself as 'strategy consultants' we should understand that their fees are going to be big. If a company says that they are planning to make a 'strategic acquisition' it means that they are going to pay far too much for something, and so on.

Strategy is a grand, heavy-sounding concept. But the best thing a leader can do in terms of strategy is demystify it and simplify it, so that the rest of the organization can understand what it is all about.

Just do it

Ok, it's time for the third and (I promise) final appearance for Herb Kelleher in this book. The co-founder and later CEO of Southwest Airlines, said . . . do you remember? 'Strategy is over-rated and doing stuff is under-rated. Our strategy? Doing stuff.' Admirably succinct. But it probably cannot be the final word. Some serious thinking has to go on before a vague plan of action or general intention can be considered a true strategy.

Alastair Campbell was famously the director of communications for Prime Minister Tony Blair. But his full job title included the word strategy, and as a strategist he is perhaps somewhat under-rated. He offered his own nine-point formula for strategic planning in the magazine *PR Week* a few years ago. It's really rather good:

1. OST is my first rule: objective, strategy, tactics. Get these the wrong way around and you are in trouble.

2. It is not a strategy unless it is written down.

3. Developing a strategy is about having arguments, not avoiding them.

4. Strategy is a team game and works best when everyone from the boardroom down to reception supports it.

5. The best strategies can be written as a word, phrase, paragraph, page, speech and book.

6. Good strategy is based on thorough analysis and understanding.

7. Good strategy is about action, not theory.

8. Communications are a means to an end – think about the business goal, not just the communications goal.

9. The best strategies are consistent, but have flexibility to adapt.[77]

Point 4 is absolutely crucial. Strategy is a team game. Which is another reason why the ancient Greek origins of the word can throw us off the scent. Strategy should not be imposed top down, with a grateful organization supposedly accepting it unquestioningly and lapping it up like loyal puppies. Strategy should be developed by involving people from all levels in the business. The 'shop floor' or 'customer-facing' perspective counts for a great deal – not least for pointing out if leaders are describing the real world or some fantasy version of it. These are the people who are going to have to put the strategy into effect. So you might as well get their view on it as soon as possible. When leadership teams go away into the countryside only to reappear at work with a shiny new strategy that no one else has been asked to comment on, that's when bad things happen.

More than academic

Of course, the subject of strategy has attracted the attention of some powerful academic minds over the years. Professor Richard Rumelt, of the Anderson School of Management at the University of California in Los Angeles, showed in *Good Strategy, Bad Strategy: The Difference and Why It Matters* that you first have to understand what it is you are really trying to do.

Strategy is not a 'superficial restatement of the obvious combined with a generous sprinkling of buzzwords,' he wrote. It should be 'a coherent plan to tackle a defined problem'.

Here are some of his other rather good observations. Good strategy is rare. Many organizations which claim to have a strategy do not. Instead, they have a set of performance goals. Or, worse, a set of vague aspirations. 'Bad strategy' occurs when there is bad doctrine, when hard choices are avoided, and/or when leaders are unwilling or unable to define and explain the nature of the challenge. The poorer a firm's resource base, the more it must depend upon adroit and clever co-ordination of actions. Competitors do not always respond quickly, nor do customers always see the value of an offering. Good strategy anticipates and exploits inertia. Changes in technology, law, costs and buyer tastes are normally beyond the control of any competitor, but they can be harnessed. (In other words – luck really matters.) [78]

Which other academic voices are worth listening to on this subject? The former dean of the Rotman School of Management at the University of Toronto, Roger Martin, co-authored a book with the former CEO of Procter and Gamble AG Lafley, called *Playing to Win*, which is a very useful strategy handbook.[79]

Forming an intelligent strategy involves making good choices, Martin and Lafley say. You have to choose when you must compete head on, when it would be better to collaborate, and when you should leave the [playing] field to others.

And Henry Mintzberg, professor at McGill University in Montreal, has also been an effective (and sceptical) analyst of this topic for years. In his book *The Rise and Fall of Strategic Planning* he dismissed 'the pronouncement of platitudes – ostensible strategies that no one has any intention of implementing, even if that were possible.'[80]

In his later work *Strategy Bites Back* (co-authored with Joe Lampel and Bruce Ahlstrand), Mintzberg criticized strategies for being 'standard, generic, uninspiring'. 'Strategy doesn't only have to position, it has to inspire,' he wrote. 'So an uninspiring strategy is really no strategy at all.'[81]

Demystify and simplify

Good strategies should ultimately be simple to explain, as Alastair Campbell argues. They need to be demystified. Indeed, although the word itself is old, it only became more widely used in the second half of the twentieth century. Before that the term 'planning' was more popular. Strategy in business was really 'invented' by the elite management consultancies. In the 1960s, firms such as McKinsey and the Boston Consulting Group elevated unglamorous planning into something much grander – strategy. And, as John Kay says, strategy was something you could build a mystique around and charge a lot more money for.

We should lighten up about strategy. The world is changing fast. You have to adapt. Strategies will have to be adjusted and rewritten. In the end it's what you do and how you do it that counts.

Vision

In 1993, the great US corporation IBM, the Big Blue, was on its knees and facing disaster. It had just registered losses of $8 billion. Its share price had sunk. A new CEO, Lou Gerstner, was brought in to help lead a rescue mission. And as analysts and employees waited to hear how Gerstner was going to start this process of recovery, he made a gloriously unexpected and down to earth observation. 'The last thing IBM needs right now is a vision,' he said.[82]

This was a bold statement. In Hollywood, and in the dreams of some corporate executives, magical visions can help transform any situation through sheer force of will. A heroic leader appears over the horizon, pronounces a Vision, clicks his or her fingers, and voila – rapid success. Life is more complicated than that, but it does not stop people 'holding out for a hero', as Bonnie Tyler used to sing.

Gerstner was right. He held the business together, and helped to shift the culture that was dragging the business down. Of course, this route to survival was the embodiment of a kind of vision, but it was one based on practical action, not unrealistic dreams.

A sceptic calls

Don Sull, senior lecturer at the MIT Sloan School of Management, has been a long-standing sceptic about the role of grand visions. Vision can become tunnel vision, he has argued, meaning that leaders stick too long with a view of the future that is being eroded by changing circumstances they do not wish to see. For example, Microsoft was slow to recognize the importance of the internet, sticking for too long on its 'a PC on every desk' vision.

As Dr Sull has written: 'A clear vision can also lull managers and employees into believing that they live in a predictable world. Employees often crave certainty in a changing industry and demand a clear vision from the top. The consequences of giving them what they want, however, can be disastrous.'[83]

This is all true. And yet a sense of vision, by which we might mean having the imagination to foresee a new and different world, is a skill leaders need to display. Some people who have visions are regarded as eccentric or possibly even unwell. So visions need to be grounded in reality, or not so far detached from it as to be meaningless fantasy.

Don Sull sets a few tests that any useful or meaningful vision has to pass. First, don't take too long over them. 'Large investments of time, energy or consultants' fees to craft the "perfect" vision statement rarely repay the effort,' he argues. If you can't explain it simply, and sum it up quickly, then maybe this great vision of yours is not so great after all.

The vision should also be specific to the industry you are in (an echo of Roger Martin and AG Lafley's view on strategic choices). 'A long-term vision should define where the company competes,' Sull says. 'This helps managers and employees to sort opportunities in their domain from those that distract them from their core business.'

More important for leaders, Sull says, is 'setting the right priorities to achieve their vision and executing more effectively and quickly than their rivals. In the end, it is these abilities, rather than any good or bad decisions they make over mission statements, that spell the difference between success and failure.'

Lack of vision

What happens when leaders have no vision at all? This can be just as bad as having the wrong vision. At time of writing, UK is wrestling with what a post-Brexit existence might look like, but the uncertainty and lack of vision at the top are proving unsettling to say the least. 'Where there is no vision the people perish,' it says in the Bible (Proverbs 29:18). We must hope that this outcome can be avoided.

Populist politicians offer grossly over-simplified visions, which nonetheless can resonate for a time and help them win elections. Donald Trump's cry of 'Make America great again!' may have been wrong-headed and misleading, but it helped to garner support. Similarly, during the UK's EU referendum earlier on in 2016, the Leave campaign promised that a vote for them would allow people to 'take back control'. Exactly what this might mean was never specified, but as a slogan it proved to be, literally, a vote winner.

Citizens and employees are wisely wary of grand visions, or of demagogues who promise the earth but leave only chaos behind them. Given visions like that, it's no wonder if some people prefer modest incrementalism and only limited ambitions.

But without a sense of something bigger and better being possible hope itself can be extinguished. Life becomes a Sisyphean task in which, contrary to Albert Camus' suggestion, the people are not happy at all. We have to raise our sights a bit – 'eyes on the stars, feet on the ground', as Teddy Roosevelt said.

Leaders who are worth following have vision. They can see further ahead. They have imagination. They aspire, and dream. These need not be crazy visions, or fantastical ones that can never be realized. When President Obama told US citizens 'Yes, we can', he gave them hope and a positive vision of the future. How many US citizens would vote to bring some of that hope back now?

As the character called Bloody Mary sings to Lieutenant Joe Cable in the Rodgers and Hammerstein musical *South Pacific*: 'If you don't have a dream, how you gonna have a dream come true?'

Some visions are worth entertaining at least for a while. Life would be very dull and unproductive without them. To be a better leader indulge your visions, for a limited period, and share them. Just be ready to move on quickly if that vision cannot be realized.

7:

A FEW IMPORTANT LEADERS

Jeff Bezos

The Amazon founder and boss may not always be the smartest guy in the room, but he is probably right up there. His success tells you that intelligence does matter, along with persistence, nerve and timing.

He did not start out in life with any particular material advantage. He was born in Albuquerque, New Mexico, in 1964. And he was smart. Frustrated by his grandmother's persistent smoking, but unwilling simply to plead for her to stop, he did a little mathematical calculation. After she'd finished another cigarette he told her: 'You've taken nine years off your life!' Upset, his grandmother cried. His grandfather took him to one side and said: 'Jeff, one day you'll understand that it's harder to be kind than clever.'[84]

Grandpa identified a tension that has run through his life and career. After getting a top degree at Princeton in electrical engineering and computer science he found himself, as a lot of people did in the late 1980s and early 90s, working in finance on Wall Street.

By 1994, aged thirty, he was a senior vice president at an investment bank called DE Shaw & Co. He was already quite rich but not what you might call satisfied. And then he heard about this thing called the internet, and started having ideas about what he might do with it.

As he later explained in a speech at Princeton given in 2010: 'I came across the fact that web usage was growing at 2,300 per cent per year. I'd never seen or heard of anything that grew that fast,' he said. 'That's huge – nothing usually grows that fast outside a petri dish.'[85]

Bezos weighed up his options, studying several different retail markets, but chose books as the field to operate in. 'The idea of building an online bookstore with millions of titles ... was very exciting to me,' he explained.[86] Books were the ideal 'battering ram' product for the new business – they were cheap, portable and sellable.

Bezos left Wall Street and went to Seattle, and started up his new online bookshop with five others in a garage. Amazon.com formally launched in July 1995.

It has been a sensational success story, branching out into most other product markets ('the everything store') and crucially selling lucrative IT services (Amazon Web Services). Currently, Amazon employs more than 300,000 people worldwide. Bezos' Alexa virtual assistant is spreading fast. Like Elon Musk, another billionaire, Bezos is into space travel. His company Blue Origin is developing a re-usable passenger rocket.

Bezos bought the *Washington Post* newspaper in 2013 for $250 million. He is also looking at developing what he calls 'affordable healthcare' with the investor Warren Buffett. Bezos owns 16 per cent of Amazon's shares and is worth over $100 billion.

His story and his success are not unambiguous. Amazon is amazingly, perhaps monstrously powerful. It is killing a lot of retail competition and changing the way we live and shop. For such a vast and successful beast it does not always seem to pay a lot of tax.

And as an employer it has a patchy record to say the least. Its 'fulfilment centres' are operated by a mixture of robots and people, both working very hard without many breaks, and the pay is not great. A major exposé of the stresses Amazon employees at all levels are under was published by the *New York Times* in 2015, which caused a serious rethink at HQ.[87]

Nonetheless, Bezos is a compelling figure as a leader because he has clearly got so much right, and in his own way. He backed a hunch. He kept going when others mocked or failed to understand him. He insists on ruthless innovation. And he follows up some of his boldest statements with a loud and apparently sincere guffaw.

Amazon must remain what he calls a 'Day One company', he says. This means they must take nothing for granted, not get stale and keep striving for more. His attention to detail is extreme. He insists on meetings remaining small, focused and businesslike. You should never need more than two pizzas to feed everyone present.

He is armed with data, but he also trusts his gut feelings. He remains action-focused. 'I don't want to be eighty years old and in a quiet moment of reflection, thinking back over my life and cataloguing a bunch of major regrets,' he has said. 'In most cases, our biggest regrets turn out to be acts of omission. It's paths not taken, and they haunt us. We wonder what would have happened.' His test is: 'What does your heart say?'[88]

But how does he lead? In his 2017 letter to shareholders, Bezos revealed the combination of intelligence married with a certain humility which has helped build the company's remarkable success. He does not pretend to know everything, nor claim to be the know-all who must have ultimate authority on any big decision.

'Most decisions should probably be made with somewhere around 70 per cent of the information you wish you had,' he wrote. 'If you wait for 90 per cent, in most cases, you're probably being slow.' Bezos advises,

Use the phrase 'disagree and commit'. This phrase will save a lot of time. If you have conviction on a particular direction even though there's no consensus, it's helpful to say, 'Look, I know we disagree on this but will you gamble with me on it? Disagree and commit?' By the time you're at this point, no one can know the answer for sure, and you'll probably get a quick yes.

This isn't one way. If you're the boss, you should do this too. I disagree and commit all the time. We recently greenlit a particular Amazon Studios original [TV production]. I told the team my view: debatable whether it would be interesting enough, complicated to produce, the business terms aren't that good, and we have lots of other opportunities. They had a completely different opinion and wanted to go ahead. I wrote back right away with 'I disagree and commit and hope it becomes the most watched thing we've ever made.' Consider how much slower this decision cycle would have been if the team had actually had to convince me rather than simply get my commitment.

Note what this example is not: it's not me thinking to myself 'well, these guys are wrong and missing the point, but this isn't worth me chasing.' It's a genuine disagreement of opinion, a candid expression of my view, a chance for the team to weigh my view, and a quick, sincere commitment to go their way. And given that this team has already brought home 11 Emmys, 6 Golden Globes, and 3 Oscars, I'm just glad they let me in the room at all![89]

Amazon is almost too successful, will be targeted by tax officials and may eventually get broken up. But Bezos has helped create one of the most powerful businesses in history, and it is still going strong – even though it has only just started making a profit after more than twenty years.

No wonder he laughs like that.

Geoffrey Canada, president and former CEO of the Harlem Children's Zone

As a young boy, Geoffrey Canada cried when his mother told him there was no such person as Superman. Who then would come and save him from his tough life in the South Bronx? Young Geoffrey resolved to try and do it for himself.[90]

He left Harlem to go to high school in Freeport, near Long Island, and eventually got a degree in psychology and sociology before entering the Harvard Graduate School of Education. After graduating, he taught first in a school for troubled youth in Boston, Massachusetts, eventually returning to Harlem in 1983 to work for the Rheedlen Institute's truancy prevention programme. In 1990 he was appointed director of Rheedlen, which he renamed the Harlem Children's Zone.

The HCZ has transformed lives, offering not just a safety

net but a springboard to greater educational and lifetime achievement. More controversially, Canada has also been a driving force in the so-called 'charter schools' movement – an inspiration for 'free schools' in the UK – where head teachers are free to deploy their own methods within a publicly funded school system, and can refuse to co-operate with teaching unions. By Canada's own admission, the track record of charter schools has been mixed, a pattern repeated with free schools in the UK. (The schools within the HCZ are massively oversubscribed, however.)

The HCZ has been a remarkable success story, and as Paul Harris described it for the *Observer* newspaper, 'while 1,400 children go to charter schools, another 8,000 benefit from Children's Zone programmes, such as after-school lessons. In short, the HCZ is far more than just a charter school group and more like an aid organization rebuilding a community.' [91]

Canada has been an inspiration to many. 'We will not let you fail' is his watchword. He has offered tough but compassionate leadership. Nine out of ten of his students now go to college and graduate. President Obama saluted his work as 'an all-encompassing, all-hands-on-deck, anti-poverty effort that is literally saving a generation of children'.

In a TED talk in 2013, Canada set out the passionately held views which have driven him on:

America cannot wait another fifty years to get this right. We have run out of time. I don't know about a fiscal cliff, but I know there's an educational cliff that we are walking over right this very second, and if we allow folks to continue this foolishness about saying we can't afford this . . . Bill Gates says it's going to cost five billion dollars. What is five billion dollars to the United States? What did we spend in Afghanistan this year? How many trillions?

When the country cares about something, we'll spend a trillion dollars without blinking an eye. When the safety of America is threatened, we will spend any amount of money. The real safety of our nation is preparing this next generation so that they can take our place and be the leaders of the world when it comes to thinking and technology and democracy and all that stuff we care about. I dare say it's a pittance, what it would require for us to really begin to solve some of these problems. [92]

In 2014 Canada announced that, at the age of sixty-two, he would be stepping down as CEO to hand over to his former COO, Anne Williams-Isom. But his remains a voice on education and reform that is listened to intently the world over.

Ken Frazier

Ken Frazier is an exceptional chief executive. He is the first black CEO of a major global pharmaceutical company – Merck – and one of only three black CEOs in the *Fortune* 500. He grew up in a tough neighbourhood in Philadelphia, and lost his mother at an early age.

In an interview with the *Harvard Business Review* (HBR), he explained how he had benefited from being bussed across town to go to school in a more prosperous part of the city, a privilege which led ultimately to his getting a law degree from Harvard. 'If you grew up in a neighbourhood like mine, you were forced to decide early on what you stood for in life, because there were a lot of peer pressures that could take you the wrong way,' he said.[93]

As a young lawyer in Philadelphia he found he still had a lot of work to do to get established.

I had to become more 'user-friendly' for partners and clients who were not prepared to understand who I really was or where I came from. I'm not saying that's fair, but learning how to get along with people who are different has been a critical success factor in my life . . . People are successful in the legal profession not just because of their skills but because they have relationships of trust and confidence. You don't get those relationships if people are not at ease with you.

Frazier defended Merck in its legal battle over the controversial Vioxx drug. He rose to become senior general counsel and executive vice president, and in 2011 was named CEO.

His period at the top of the business has been a success. There has been a renewed commitment to research and development, and new drugs have come on stream, not least Keytruda, which helps patients suffering with lung cancer.

But Frazier would have remained a relatively low-profile boss if he had not, in the summer of 2017, appalled by President Trump's response to the neo-Nazi marches in Charlottesville, Virginia, chosen to resign from the President's manufacturing council, with the full support of his board.[94]

Frazier said: 'America's leaders must honour our fundamental values by clearly rejecting expressions of hatred, bigotry, and group supremacy . . . as a matter of personal conscience, I feel a responsibility to take a stand against intolerance and extremism.'

Trump's classy, tweeted response? 'He will have more time TO LOWER RIPOFF DRUG PRICES!'

For a day or two, few other CEOs spoke out in support of Frazier's stance. As one told the *New York Times*: 'Just look at what he [Trump] did to Ken. I'm not sticking my head up.' Which is a funny way of showing leadership.

Frazier explained the thinking behind his move to HBR:

When I saw what had happened in Charlottesville and when I heard the comments that had been made, I felt a strong conviction that by not taking action I would be endorsing what had happened and what had been said. I asked my board for its endorsement, because I wanted to speak to the company's values as well as my own. I didn't expect it to have the ripple effect it did.

I didn't see this as a political issue. It's an issue that goes to our fundamental values as a country. We aspire to be a rational, tolerant, hopefully enlightened collection of free people. We don't all look the same. We don't come from the same countries. What we share are the ideals that make the United States unique.

But perhaps his principled stand should not have come as a surprise. Frazier's long-term, values-based approach to leadership and management have not been a secret. As he told HBR:

While a fundamental responsibility of business leaders is to create value for shareholders, I think businesses also exist to deliver value to society. Merck has existed for

126 years; its individual shareholders have turned over countless times. But our salient purpose in the world is to deliver medically important vaccines and medicines that make a huge difference for humanity. The revenue and shareholder value we create are an imperfect proxy for the value we create for patients and society.

And his tweet-length version of that answer? 'Keep your eyes on the prize. Manage to the long term, not to what Wall Street says it wants in the short term.'

The final advantage Frazier enjoys is a certain modesty and humility about his role as a leader. His words in the same HBR interview are also worth reproducing:

CEOs have to be willing to give up power. The most important decisions made inside Merck are not made in my office.

The most significant levers CEOs have are to put the right people in leadership positions and to ensure that the incentives inside the company are aligned so that people are working toward a common purpose. Leaders need to be purpose-driven, not personality-driven. If you don't believe in your company's intrinsic value or its contribution to society, if you're just focused on trying to make money, you're not going to be successful in the long run.

The ultimate test of a leader is: who are the people who will take over from you, and are they as talented and as committed as they need to be to succeed?

You have to fight against hierarchy, which is one of the biggest obstacles to success and innovation. It's important for leaders to diffuse power to people who are actually in a position to make a difference. I'd love to convince Merck's people that they already know what to do – that they don't need to look up to their leaders for answers.

No wonder Trump hates him. They have absolutely nothing in common.

Mary Barra

General Motors was one of the US's greatest corporations. It brought us the Cadillac, the Chevrolet, the Hummer and the Pontiac, among other marques. It was a symbol of all-conquering US business. One of its bosses once declared: 'What's good for the country is good for General Motors, and vice versa.'

GM was also the inspiration for the most important management writer of them all, Peter Drucker. He spent two years with the company in the 1940s when it was being run by Alfred Sloan. This extended study period provided the source material for Drucker's influential book *Concept of the Corporation*.[95]

GM was the nearest the US got to having corporate royal family. Which is why it was so shocking in 2008/9 that, after years of struggle, the company needed to be bailed out (along with Chrysler) with government money, to the tune of $13.4 billion in financing from TARP (Troubled Assets Relief Program) funds.

A new, slimmed down General Motors emerged from the debris, and in January 2014 a GM lifer, Mary Barra, became the company's first female CEO. And just two months into her tenure the company finally revealed that a faulty ignition problem, which the company had known about for years, had probably been responsible for several fatalities. (The fault led to the loss of power steering and the failure of air bags to open when needed.)

GM recalled 2.6 million cars in the first instance. Cynics wondered whether the impossible task of cleaning up the company had been handed to a woman – a classic 'glass cliff' appointment.

In the summer of 2014, Barra was summoned to appear before a Senate hearing. She impressed some observers with her plain talking and relative candour. 'My name is Mary Barra, and I am the chief executive officer of General Motors,' was how she began. Followed by: 'I am deeply sorry.'

Barra insisted that GM's internal investigation should uncover all the facts. An uncapped compensation fund was set up to pay victims of the mechanical failure. The company ultimately recalled over 20 million vehicles. As many as 124 deaths may have been caused by the faulty ignition problem, costing the firm GM hundreds of millions of dollars in compensation.

Barra is an engineer with an MBA from the Stanford Graduate School of Business. She has the right pedigree to lead. And a blog post she wrote in January 2015, after she had begun the clear-up, is quite revealing about how she has approached the job. She wrote:

I've been fortunate to spend my entire career with one company, General Motors, which has never failed to challenge me or offer opportunities for growth. And yet, within GM, I've held more than a dozen different positions in everything from engineering and manufacturing to communications and human resources.[96]

An important principle for her is that she and other leaders should 'take personal responsibility':

If you inherit a problem with your new job, don't dismiss it as the last person's legacy. Never hide behind your newbie status or use it as an excuse to put off what needs to be done. Own the problem, develop a plan to fix it, and address it head on. Your team's reputation depends not just on what you do right, but what you do if something goes wrong.

She seems to be making it all work. Between 2013 and 2016, GM profits per share doubled. She has continued a process of modernization and simplification while preparing for a very different future for the business and the industry. Her soundbite is that 'the next five years will see more change than the last fifty years.'

GM has cut costs, reduced some US production and retreated from less profitable markets. It sold its Opel and Vauxhall brands to PSA Group (Peugeot) and also pulled out of India and South Africa.

But it is also looking ahead. GM spent more than $1 billion to buy Cruise, a San Francisco 'autonomous vehicle' start-up. They also spent $500 million investing in Lyft, the rival to Uber, and also launched its own car-sharing service, Maven.

Barra has shattered one of the thickest and obstinate of glass ceilings, by taking the reins of a venerable industrial beast, and doing a good job. If the car industry has a future it will be because of the insightful leadership of people like Mary Barra.

Indra Nooyi

When a leader announces her departure after a twelve-year stint at the top, and it still comes as a bit of a surprise, it's a sign that this is a leader who was in full command until the last minute. Such was the reaction in August 2018 when Indra Nooyi, CEO of PepsiCo, said she would step down in Spring 2019. I had long been an admirer. Her many qualities were on display around a decade ago, when she came in for a lunch at the *Financial Times*, where I was working as the management columnist. She was a bright and breezy lunch guest, confident, approachable and informal. I'm not sure that many of the gentlemen in the room – and it was an almost entirely male group – had ever met a CEO quite like this before.

Nooyi set out her aims for the company in clear terms. If PepsiCo was going to have a future it would have to recognize that some of its products (fizzy drinks, crisps, orange juice) contained ingredients – sugar, for example, and fat – which should not be consumed to excess. PepsiCo was going to have to achieve 'performance with purpose', she told us. She aimed to recalibrate its product range into three categories: 'fun for you' (the naughty stuff), 'better for you' (reduced quantities of sugar/fat), and 'good for you' (actually healthy stuff).

Not everyone, inside or outside the room, was immediately convinced by this pitch. Certainly mainstream investors kept up pressure on the company, with some suggesting that rather than saving the world or our health they should really be selling more cans of fizzy pop.

But Nooyi was undaunted. Products didn't just have to

pass the CEO test or the market test, she said, they had to 'pass the mommy test' – Nooyi has two children.

I was convinced. Not least when – even though she was in the middle of a long answer to another colleague – she broke off to note that I had greedily reached into a bag of wheaty snacks her people had distributed round the room. 'You like them, huh?!' she observed. Well, it had been a long time since breakfast. Too long, also, for another colleague, who began eating before the CEO had been served her lunch. Again, she took the embarrassed apology graciously.

A decade on, Nooyi was still in place at PepsiCo, having ridden out recession and some persistent carping from parts of the market. At the time of writing, PepsiCo is said to be a potential bid target for the Kraft corporation (a predator seen off by Paul Polman and Unilever in 2017). Something must have gone very right at PepsiCo during the twelve years Nooyi spent as CEO.

The only sadness from a parochial, British point of view is that Nooyi could have made her career in the UK. She grew up in Chennai (then Madras), India, and after a masters degree at Yale in the US the opportunity existed for her to build a career in Britain. But America proved more attractive. And after a few years in consulting with Booz Allen Hamilton, and then a corporate career at Motorola and Asea Brown Boveri, she joined PepsiCo in 1994, becoming CFO in 2001 and CEO five years later. She was an all too rare female CEO of a major corporation.

Nooyi says she followed some advice her mother gave her on how to behave at home with the rest of the family: 'leave the crown in the garage'.[97] It is certainly true that the imperial CEO – with staff, every logistical need taken care of, first-class travel and accommodation – can get cut off from the banal quotidian requirements of life. This is bad enough for any CEO, but for the boss of company selling competitively priced, fast-moving consumer goods it could be disastrous.

Perhaps it is this down-to-earth quality, combined with a first-class brain, which provided the foundation for Nooyi's success. She remained 100 per cent human even while helping to steer one of the world's great corporations in uncertain times. She has passed the mommy test as well as the CEO test.

Paul Polman, former CEO, Unilever

Conventional wisdom weighs heavily in business. Some ideas, even when they can be shown not to be working terribly well, can prove hard to shift. In those circumstances it takes courage to go against the grain.

The concept of 'maximizing shareholder value' is one such dubious but resilient idea. In short, the theory is that public companies should be run to generate the biggest possible returns to shareholders, preferably as quickly as possible. All that nice talk about long termism is all very well, but if the dividends aren't looking too healthy for a quarter or two, your time as CEO could be up quite soon. So CEOs are supposed to talk enthusiastically about shareholder value and sound as though they mean what they are saying.

Which makes it all the remarkable that Paul Polman, who became CEO of Unilever in 2009 and immediately declared shareholder value to be a bad idea, was still in his job almost a decade later. He told the hedge funds to clear off, along with any other shareholder who was looking for a fast buck. As he told me in an interview for the *Financial Times* in 2010:

> I do not work for the shareholder, to be honest; I work for the consumer, the customer . . . I discovered a long time ago that if I focus on doing the right thing for the long term to improve the lives of consumers and customers all over the world, the business results will come . . . I drive this business model by focusing on the consumer and customer in a responsible way, and I know that shareholder value can come.
>
> It's easy to be a short-term hero. It is very easy for me to get tremendous results very short term, get that translated into compensation and be off sailing in the Bahamas. But the goal for this company – and it's very difficult to do – the goal is to follow a four or five year process. We need to change the strategy and the structure as well as the culture.[98]

These kinds of pronouncements were met with great scepticism when Polman first made them, from all over the financial press and the investment industry. It represented a bold challenge to conventional wisdom at the time. There was much muttering along the lines of 'they'll get you for this'.

Polman finally stepped down at the end of 2018. The nearest Polman came to being ousted was when Kraft came gunning for Unilever in an ill-judged takeover bid in 2017. The bid was repulsed quite easily. Today more shareholders than before are long-term holders of Unilever stock. He and his colleagues bucked the trend for short termism, even when people told them they were crazy to try.

What form did Polman's courage take? He helped develop what the company called its Sustainable Living Plan, an ambitious idea to use fewer and fewer natural resources while still building up the company's sales and profitability.

And, give or take, that is exactly what happened under Polman's leadership. The share price has doubled since I interviewed him at the start of the decade. 'Total shareholder return' has been high, above that produced by Procter and Gamble (where Polman worked for twenty-seven years) and Nestlé (where he worked for three years as chief financial officer before taking over at Unilever in 2009).

Polman's leadership was groundbreaking. He is a serious man, born in 1956, the second of six children in a Catholic Dutch family. He was a demanding boss for the company, but also very clear about what they should be trying to achieve. His was a model of purposeful leadership. He provided a story (narrative) which employees could understand and believe in.

In another *FT* piece he was quoted as claiming that Unilever is a kind of NGO (non-governmental organization, or charity).[99] That is pushing it a bit. But he managed to convey a sense of mission or cause.

Profitability with purpose has long been a dream of progressive business types, and campaigners. No one has got closer to realizing this ideal on a grand scale than Unilever's Paul Polman and his team.

His approach has also won the approval of academic commentators. Colin Mayer, professor of management studies at Oxford University's Saïd Business School, told the *FT*: 'He has demonstrated immense courage and vision in promoting a concept of the purpose and function of business that initially met with considerable resistance, bordering on hostility, from several quarters.'

Not every PLC boss can be like Paul Polman. But the world would be a much better place if they were.

Rosa Parks

Leadership is not necessarily a question of issuing instructions or placing yourself at the top of a hierarchy. You can also display leadership in the choices you make or through your behaviour. If you take a stand others may follow. You will have become a leader without even intending to.

Rosa Parks did not know, when she boarded the bus to go home in Montgomery, Alabama, on 1 December 1955, that this bus journey was about to change history. She was a forty-two-year-old seamstress, married to a fellow active supporter of the NAACP (National Association for the Advancement of Colored People). She had finished a day's work, and took her seat in the 'colored' section on the bus (behind the first four rows of seats, which were reserved for white people – this was how segregation worked at that time).

As the bus continued on its route it filled up with passengers. After a time, the driver noticed that some white passengers were standing. He moved the sign indicating where black people should sit back a row and told four passengers to stand and give up their seats. Three agreed. Parks did not.

'Why don't you stand up?' the driver asked her. 'I don't think I should have to stand up,' she replied. The police were called. Parks was arrested and charged with a violation of

Chapter 6, Section 11 segregation law of the Montgomery City code, and released on bail later that evening.

Three days later, on Sunday 4 December, the Montgomery Bus Boycott was launched through announcements made in churches. Organizers had produced 35,000 handbills to publicize it. The protest would involve black residents boycotting the buses until basic courtesy was extended to them as passengers, seats in the middle of the bus were available to all, and black bus drivers were hired.

The campaigners asked their black fellow citizens to boycott the buses on that first Monday, 5 December and, although it rained, tens of thousands did. The boycott was kept up for 381 days, hitting the bus company's finances as their vehicles stood idle, and causing a national sensation.

Eventually the city of Montgomery was forced to give in and end the enforcement of segregation on its buses. The protest ended on 20 December 1956. A massive blow had been struck against the principle of racial segregation in America's south.

In an interview on National Public Radio several decades later, Rosa Parks explained that she had not foreseen how her individual protest might produce such significant consequences.

I did not want to be mistreated, I did not want to be deprived of a seat that I had paid for. It was just time. There was opportunity for me to take a stand to express the way I felt about being treated in that manner. I had not planned to get arrested. I had plenty to do without having to end up in jail. But when I had to face that decision, I didn't hesitate to do so because I felt that we had endured that too long. The more we gave in, the more we complied with that kind of treatment, the more oppressive it became.[100]

Dr Martin Luther King referred to Rosa Parks' act of leadership in his book *Stride Toward Freedom*, which was published in 1958. 'No one can understand the action of Mrs Parks unless he realizes that eventually the cup of endurance runs over, and the human personality cries out, "I can take it no longer",' he wrote.

Leadership takes courage. You can have all the best conceived strategies and plans in the world. But if you do not have the courage to enact them they will remain theoretical documents. This is what Jim Collins is getting at when he talks about the sacrifice involved in true leadership. You are putting yourself on the line. You are vulnerable and open to challenge and criticism.

There is too much talk of supposedly 'heroic' leaders with alleged superpowers or miraculous capabilities or gifts. Many of the leadership heroes we worship for a while seem to let us down in the end, when their essential normality is revealed. But sometimes people do display raw courage and leadership which changes people lives for the better. Rosa Parks was one such person.

Winston Churchill

As every reader knows, it is compulsory when writing a book about leadership to include a section on Churchill. We just can't get away from him. Although he's been dead for over fifty years he is still at the front of our minds.

In 2012, the research firm Britain Thinks found that

'Churchill remains the archetypal leader'.[101] Three years later, the same firm was even more confident in this view. As their co-founder Deborah Mattinson wrote in the *Observer* newspaper: 'Churchill is in a league of his own, head and shoulders above the rest. That's why we created the Churchill Index to see how other leaders – past and present – measure up, particularly on the top three attributes: great communication, decisiveness and integrity.'[102]

Two years later, Britain Thinks checked in with voters again, and Churchill was still top of the pops.[103] His is a reign without end.

But if you were expecting this book's compulsory Churchill section to be an unqualified eulogy or a simple hymn of praise you are in for a surprise. Churchill's story is indeed instructive for people wanting to understand how they could become a better leader. But there are several aspects to his life story which need to be considered, and the idea that he can be a role model for leadership in the twenty-first century is questionable.

There seem to be a few commonly held beliefs about the life of Churchill which are broadly true. He was born into an aristocratic family as a grandson of the seventh Duke of Marlborough. He struggled at school, where he was an erratic if occasionally brilliant pupil. He got into the Royal Military Academy at Sandhurst, Surrey, only on the third attempt. He was a brave if occasionally reckless young soldier, and a politician with mixed success, capable of both compassionate insights and callous cruelty. He miscalculated badly during the First World War, and again subsequently as chancellor of the exchequer, with huge cost in human life and livelihoods. By the 1930s, in his early sixties, he was seen as a maverick, marginal and perhaps rather untrustworthy figure. He denounced Soviet Communism and, as a British imperialist, opposed the fight for independence in India. His warnings about the growing threat of Nazism in Germany were rejected by the government of the day.

And then the Second World War started, Prime Minister Chamberlain fell, and Churchill took command. He made great speeches, called for 'action this day', formed a powerful new alliance with the once hated Soviets, and helped lead Britain to victory with its US and Soviet allies. He helped 'save the free world' it is often said, and became the paradigm for leadership which, as the survey data on the previous page suggest, holds to this day. In Britain and America he is seen, usually uncontroversially, as a great leader. That is partly why films like *Darkest Hour* keep getting made, and why aspiring and ambitious politicians (and other leaders) obsess about him or aim to emulate him.

And yet. In 1919, as secretary of state for war, Churchill advocated using what he called 'lachrymatory gas'. 'I am strongly in favour of using poisoned gas against uncivilised tribes,' he wrote in a memo. 'The moral effect should be so good that the loss of life should be reduced to a minimum. It is not necessary to use only the most deadly gasses: gasses can be used which cause great inconvenience and would spread a lively terror and yet would leave no serious permanent effects on most of those affected.'[104]

As a younger man witnessing fighting in the sub-continent of India, Churchill had mused openly in his writings about how the British were a 'superior race', while at other times in his military and political career, in Kenya, in Afghanistan and modern-day Pakistan, Churchill supported actions or championed behaviour that would be regarded as criminal and wholly unacceptable today.

His role in the Bengal famine of 1943, it is argued by some historians, led to the death of millions. In her book *Churchill's Secret War*, Madhusree Mukerjee says that while Indians starved, the British kept prices high and surplus grain was exported. Australian ships were not allowed to unload their cargo of wheat in Calcutta. Churchill ordered that grain be shipped to increase stocks ahead of a possible future invasion of Greece and Yugoslavia.[105]

If we consider Churchill's war-time leadership – with the exception of the Bengal famine – then you can see why his popular reputation, in much of the western world, remains intact. His qualities of 'great communication, decisiveness and integrity', as outlined in the Britain Thinks research, hold good. Even the brutal, heavy bombing of civilians in Dresden has been justified as part of a 'total war' that was not of Britain's making. The Second World War was a just war to defeat fascism and for national survival, and Churchill led his country well.

But consider too that only weeks after Victory in Europe day in May 1945, Churchill's governing Conservatives were dumped humiliatingly out of office by Labour's landslide general election victory. And if you still find it hard to believe that the people's hero could be kicked out in this way so soon after the war, check out the newsreel footage of Churchill being booed and heckled at Walthamstow stadium that summer – startling indeed.

An American journalist called Ralph Ingersoll made the essential point in his reporting from London in 1940, later published in a book called *Report on England*.[106] Here is what he said at the time:

Everywhere I went in London people admired [Churchill's] energy, his courage, his singleness of purpose. People said they didn't know what Britain would do without him. He was obviously respected. But no one felt he would be prime minister after the war. He was simply the right man in the right job at the right time. The time being the time of a desperate war with Britain's enemies.

The right person at the right time – that was Churchill between 1940 and 1945. We have much to learn from him and what he did in those circumstances. But few of us will ever face a leadership challenge like his. And so today's latter-day, wannabe Churchills probably need to calm down just a bit and concentrate on the task in hand.

8:

SO YOU (STILL) WANT TO BE A LEADER?

Believe in something (and other people)

You need a certain kind of confidence – arrogance, even – to call yourself a leader. It implies that you possess some rare or superior gifts. And maybe you do. But leadership without beliefs or purpose is empty, mere demagoguery or vanity. If you want your leadership to mean something and have value you had better believe in something.

The actor Michael Sheen put it well in a passionate speech he gave on St David's day, 1 March 2015, in the middle of a British general election campaign. He was exasperated at the carefully pre-prepared, neutral, inoffensive and sterile comments that political leaders were coming up with. He wanted something more raw and more honest: 'There is never an excuse to not speak up for what you think is right,' he declared. 'You must stand up for what you believe. But first of all – by God, believe in something.'[107]

Ambition is necessary, but selfish ambition alone, for material riches or status, is unlikely to inspire others. Leadership has to be about contribution, not just taking rewards out of the business. So if you are asking people to make sacrifices – disruption to their family life, facing financial uncertainty – you will have to suffer too. And it is only worth suffering in a good cause. If it hurts to work where you are but there is no purpose to it you are wasting your time, and other people's.

This is the second point about belief: you should believe not just in something but in other people too. Work gets done in teams. It is a collective enterprise. One of the most damaging myths that has grown up around leadership is that it is somehow a solo activity. That it can be done on its own, regardless of others. This is the thinking – if it can be called that – which lies behind the enormous pay packets which some leaders receive. 'They are doing this on their own', the numbers seem to imply. 'They are invaluable.'

Very few leaders are invaluable, irreplaceable or indispensable. They are only human after all. Without belief, though, leaders are misrepresenting themselves to their organizations. And without recognizing the debt they owe to their people, leaders are heading down the wrong track.

Even Steve Jobs, that most dominant and forceful of leaders, had to acknowledge how much he depended on the people around him at Apple. When his biographer Walter Isaacson asked him what he thought his greatest achievement had been, Isaacson thought the answer might be the Macintosh or the iPhone. But Jobs' answer was different. 'Making a Mac or an iPhone is hard,' he said, 'but making a team that will always turn out Macs and iPhones, that's the [really] hard part.'[108]

Belief

And so to return to Jim Collins' great question to leaders and wannabe leaders: 'What are you in it for?' The answer ought to be something bigger than you or your ego. There ought to be a purpose to your leadership: the building of a legacy, the strengthening of an organization to be passed on to others. To do all this you need to believe in what you are doing and in the work you are helping others to carry out.

Set goals (for yourself and others)

You have got to aim for something. Whether it is increased market share, radical innovation or merely survival, there has got to be an end in mind. Without goals you are just clinging on or treading water, to no good purpose. You might as well pack up, sell up and go away.

Good leaders will set goals for themselves, for others and their organization. But they must be set carefully. What gets measured gets managed, it is true. But what gets managed gets manipulated. If you give people a target they will try and hit it. So think very hard when you set goals for people. Does it make sense? Is it achievable or is it just wildly unrealistic? If you are using a 'performance related pay' incentive scheme make sure you are asking people to hit worthwhile and sustainable targets.

We mentioned 'BHAGs' (Big Hairy Audacious Goals) earlier in this book (page 47). I am a bit of a sceptic about these. If a goal seems impossibly remote it can hardly be meaningful, and therefore cannot inspire. But goals can certainly be Big and quite possibly Audacious, within reason. It's the Hairiness I think we can probably do without.

Goals can be set for the short, medium and long term.

Short

Simply meeting the monthly (or weekly) pay-roll bill can be a hard enough goal when times are hard. For all the grand talk about leadership (which can be fun to wallow in and which I have probably perpetrated in the preceding pages), anyone who has not had to pay staff and suppliers regularly and on time has not experienced one of the most basic facts of leadership of all: cash is king and if you don't have enough of the stuff you are in trouble.

That said, we should not let short-term financial pressures obscure what other immediate tasks have to be completed. Customer service is a constant short-term – real time – pressure. Deadlines should be met. Sensible work hours should be observed. If people are still at work late and over weekends then the apparent 'urgency' of short-term goals is overriding the important long-term thinking which needs to go on.

Medium

I am quite taken with Sir William Sargent's view (see page 20) that the medium term can be left to worry about itself as long as both short- and long-term goals are being respected. But this might not work for everyone and every business, especially those that are not so project based. Medium-term goals can be needed to track progress. Are you on course? What adjustments are needed? You have already heard (page 56) what General Eisenhower said about plans: they will need to change. But that does not make planning and medium-term goals useless.

Long

Long-term goals are the most important of all. They are the north star, the purpose, the reason to be. They must never be forgotten and, as Sir William Sargent says, everything you do must be consistent with them. It's the acid test when you are not sure if a project makes sense. If it is consistent with the long-term purpose of your organization then it is probably ok, if resources allow for it.

Goal!

Goals help, especially when the pressure is on. Distractions can be ignored if goals still command people's attention. And goals can help colleagues keep going even if the boss is being, frankly, a pain in the arse.

If people believe in the goals of the business they are more likely to believe in you as a leader, even when you are being tough. As Steve Jobs' biographer Walter Isaacson says about his subject: 'Jobs was a deeply spiritual, very intense person who had rough edges and was nasty at times, and mean. But having driven people crazy, they'd also walk through walls for him. He'd drive them to do things that they didn't know they could do.'[109]

This is what goals can do for you, at Apple and elsewhere.

Persist

It isn't easy, leadership. You have presumably picked up this book because you recognize that, and because you have the humility to acknowledge that there could be more for you to learn about it. This bodes well. It's the leaders who think the top job represents a finishing line rather than the start of something new whom we should be worrying about.

Leadership makes demands and calls for sacrifice. It is not a popularity contest. And it takes time. Beware of so-called 'quick wins' which fail to deal with underlying problems and in fact build up the store of future problems that you will have to wrestle with.

Persistence is vital precisely because there will be few quick, important, lasting victories. You will have to communicate a message up to ten times, through a variety of channels, before colleagues are likely to have absorbed it properly, the HR guru Dave Ulrich estimates. (That is only the second time I have mentioned Ulrich's 10x theory, so you are getting off lightly. Say it to yourself another eight times to see if it's true.) You have to have a goal and stick at it, deploying what Professor John Kotter has called 'urgent patience'.

Tough-minded optimism

In his book *Simply Brilliant*, the writer Bill Taylor recalled the phrase coined by the American educationalist John Gardner: 'tough-minded optimism'. It is this sort of resilient approach, Taylor argues, that leaders need today.

Taylor set out his argument in a blog post for *Harvard Business Review*[110]. One aspect of tough-minded optimism, he said, is having the confidence and courage to stick to your guns, to be consistent and not change with every passing management fad. Taylor quoted Jim Collins: 'The signature of mediocrity is not an unwillingness to change. The signature of mediocrity is chronic inconsistency.'

Taylor drew on some further words of John Gardner: 'The future is not shaped by people who don't really believe in the future,' Gardner said. Rather, 'it is created by highly motivated people, by enthusiasts, by men and women who want something very much or believe very much.' To this Taylor added: 'The best leaders have all sorts of skills and use all kinds of techniques, but there is no substitute [for what Gardner called] "the lift of spirit and heightened performance that comes from strong motivation".'

Tough love

Walter Isaacson took part in a fascinating discussion with Adam Grant, professor at the Wharton School in Philadelphia, on the nature of leadership, creativity and learning. [111] At one point they reflected on Steve Jobs' famously abrasive, and at times extremely harsh, approach to colleagues.

Isaacson said that Jobs felt unable to glide over problems in the manner of a confident, privileged person. He saw himself as a misfit and someone who had not started out with many advantages in life. Jobs told him: 'When people do something that sucks, I have to tell them it sucks because I'm just a middle-class kid trying to make sure I don't have b-players on my team. I can't afford to be as gentle and as nice.'

Isaacson questioned this attitude. 'You don't have to be that mean,' he said. 'You don't have to be cruel to people. You have to be tough, and you have to be intellectually honest.' But, Isaacson conceded, under less abrasive leadership Apple might not have achieved all that it did.

Adam Grant noted that leaders are sometimes likened to parents, who have to be both demanding and supportive.

'He [Jobs] left out the supportive a lot, and sometimes he took the demanding way too far.'

All leaders are different in their own way. You must find your own style – 'be yourself, more, with skill', as Rob Goffee and Gareth Jones put it. But whichever style you adopt to deal with the leadership challenges you face, you will have to operate with tough-minded optimism, tough love and persistence.

Start now

You cannot think your way into a new way of acting or being. It works the other way round. Action has to come first. The title of Professor Herminia Ibarra's book *Act Like a Leader, Think Like a Leader* was worded that way deliberately. Sometimes, Ibarra says, you just have to start trying out new things, new approaches, to see if they work, and to adopt them as part of your repertoire of behaviour if they do. This is not 'fake it until you can make it', she says, but it does mean that leadership roles may make new demands on you that cannot be met by the way you used to do things or have done them until now.[112]

Develop a 'bias for action'. As a leader, your behaviour is watched and noticed. If you are active this sets the right example. One bit of Churchillian behaviour you can safely copy is the 'action this day' principle.

We cannot wait for leadership. We need it now. We always will. So, if you are a leader, and want to be a better one, right now would be a good time to start making that wish become a reality.

NOTES

All online resources accessed May 2018, unless otherwise stated.

1 Collins, J (2001) *Good to Great: Why Some Companies Make the Leap . . . And Others Don't*, William Collins, New York, NY

2 Mercer, J, Diary, *New Statesman,* 2 March 2018 https://www.newstatesman.com/world/2018/03/johnny-mercer-s-diary-macron-s-vision-may-s-problems-and-saving-nhs

3 Phillips, R, 'Davos and the Banality of Trust', *Management Today*, January 2018 https://www.managementtoday.co.uk/davos-banality-trust/reputation-matters/article/1455073

4 Cited in 'Davos and the Banality of Trust' by R Phillips, as above

5 Interview with Tim Minchin, *Guardian,* January 2018 https://www.theguardian.com/stage/2018/jan/29/it-was-unbearable-tim-minchin-on-life-under-trump-and-the-collapse-of-his-100m-movie

6 Morrison, N, 'The Secret of Exceptional Leaders' https://change-effect.com/2018/01/29/the-secret-of-exceptional-leaders/

7 Brooks, D, 'The New Power Structure', *New York Times,* 5 April 2018 https://www.nytimes.com/2018/04/05/opinion/the-new-power-structure.html

8 Knowledge at Wharton, January 2018 http://knowledge.wharton.upenn.edu/article/leadership-age-gig-economy/?utm_source=kw_newsletter&utm_medium=email&utm_campaign=2018-01-25

9   Denning, S (2004) *Squirrel, Inc – A Fable of Leadership Through Storytelling,* John Wiley & Sons, Hoboken, New Jersey

10 Elisabeth Bumiller, *New York Times*, 12 January 2004 https://www.nytimes.com/2004/01/12/us/white-house-letter-bush-gets-vision-thing-and-embraces-big-risks.html

11 Augier, M (2004) 'James March on Education, Leadership, and Don Quixote: Introduction and Interview,' *Academy of Management Learning & Education*, http://www.jstor.org/stable/40214247

12 Hill, A, *Financial Times*, https://www.ft.com/content/c81d422c-05a3-11e8-9650-9c0ad2d7c5b5

13 Goffee, R and Jones, G, *Harvard Business Review,* September 2000 https://hbr.org/2000/09/why-should-anyone-be-led-by-you

14 Goffee, R and Jones, G (2006) *Why Should Anyone Be Led By You? What It Takes to Be an Authentic Leader*, Harvard Business School Press, Boston, MA

15 Lyrics adapted by Dearmer, P. 'He who would valiant be' https://play.hymnswithoutwords.com/he-who-would-valiant-be-monks-gate/

16 Collins, J (2001) *Good to Great: Why Some Companies Make the Leap . . . And Others Don't*, William Collins, New York, NY

17 http://www.oxfordreference.com/view/10.1093/acref/9780191826719.001.0001/q-oro-ed4-00008596

18 Interview with Kelleher, *Strategy and Business*, 1 June 2004 https://www.strategy-business.com/article/04212?gko=8cb4f

19 Interview with the author

20 Murphy, P, 'Brian Clough: Pat Murphy's Memories of a Unique Character', 20 September 2004 https://www.bbc.co.uk/sport/football/29145641

21 https://hbr.org/2004/01/narcissistic-leaders-the-incredible-pros-the-inevitable-cons

22 Wolff, M, (2018) *Fire and Fury – Inside the Trump White House*, Little, Brown, New York, NY

23 Christensen, C (1997) *The Innovator's Dilemma – When New Technologies Cause Great Firms to Fail*, Harvard Business School Press, Boston, MA

24 BBC press release, 7 February 2002 http://www.bbc.co.uk/pressoffice/pressreleases/stories/2002/02_february/07/makingithappen.shtml

25 Remnick, D, 'Hope Against Hope', *New Yorker*, 28 February 2018, https://www.newyorker.com/news/news-desk/hope-hicks-against-hope

26 Kotter, J (2008) *A Sense of Urgency*, Harvard Business School Press, Boston, MA

27 https://www.tititudorancea.com/z/samuel_goldwyn_17.htm

28 Treanor, J, 'Whistleblower at HBOS Attacks "ludicrously bad" City Regulation', 14 November 2015 https://www.theguardian.com/business/2015/nov/14/whistleblower-hbos-attacks-ludicrously-bad-city-regulators-paul-moore

29 https://www.christianquotes.info/top-quotes/16-wise-christian-quotes-by-augustine/#axzz5EdY6DsKd

30 Pfeffer, J, (2010) *Power: Why Some People Have It—and Others Don't*, Harper Collins, New York, NY

31 Schawbel, D, 'Jeffrey Pfeffer: What Most People Don't Know About Leadership', *Forbes,* 15 September 2015 https://www.forbes.com/sites/danschawbel/2015/09/15/jeffrey-pfeffer-what-most-people-dont-know-about-leadership/#57fbf877ef41

32 'Kerry discusses $87 billion comment', CNN, 30 September 2004 http://edition.cnn.com/2004/ALLPOLITICS/09/30/kerry.comment/

33 http://news.bbc.co.uk/onthisday/hi/dates/stories/
october/10/newsid_2541000/2541071.stm

34 Corinthians 1, Chapter 14 verse 8

35 'Donald Trump's Hands-on Management Style to be Tested by
Presidency', AP, 26 November 2016
https://www.financialexpress.com/world-news/donald-
trumps-hands-on-management-style-to-be-tested-by-
presidency/456784/

36 Useem, M (2006) *The Go Point: When It's Time to
Decide — Knowing What to Do and When to Do It*,
Crown Business, New York, NY

37 'Michael Useem's *The Go Point: Knowing When It's Time to
Decide*', Knowledge@Wharton, 4 October 2006 http://
knowledge.wharton.upenn.edu/article/michael-useems-the-
go-point-knowing-when-its-time-to-decide/

38 https://www.sas.upenn.edu/~baron/from_cattell/humor.
html

39 Hemingway, E (1926), *The Sun Also Rises*, Scribner, New
York, NY

40 Collins, J (2001) *Good to Great: Why Some Companies
Make the Leap . . . And Others Don't*, William Collins,
New York, NY

41 Sutton, B, 25 September 2008 http://bobsutton.typepad.
com/my_weblog/2008/09/sesame-street-simple-ag-lafleys-
leadership-philosiphy.html

42 Cowdrey, L, 'Churchill Calls for Brevity', National Archives
blog,17 October 2013 http://blog.nationalarchives.gov.uk/
blog/churchills-call-for-brevity/

43 https://winstonchurchill.org/resources/speeches/1940-the-
finest-hour/blood-toil-tears-and-sweat-2/

44 Discussion with the author

45 Rosenzweig, P (2014) *Left Brain, Right Stuff – How Leaders Make Winning Decisions*, Public Affairs, New York, NY

46 Rosenzweig, P (2007) *The Halo Effect . . . And Eight Other Business Delusions That Deceive Managers*, Free Press, New York, NY

47 'Microsoft CEO Satya Nadella: How Empathy Sparks Innovation', Knowledge@Wharton, 22 February 2018 http://knowledge.wharton.upenn.edu/article/microsofts-ceo-on-how-empathy-sparks-innovation/

48 'The Work of Leadership Is the Work of Change' https://williamctaylor.com/resources/briefly-brilliant-the-work-of-leadership-is-the-work-of-change/

49 'From Leonardo da Vinci to Steve Jobs: The Benefits of Being a Misfit', Knowledge@Wharton, 17 January 2018 http://knowledge.wharton.upenn.edu/article/leonardo-da-vinci-steve-jobs-benefits-misfit/?utm_source=kw_newsletter&utm_medium=email&utm_campaign=2018-01-18

50 Letter to Amazon shareholders (2017) https://www.sec.gov/Archives/edgar/data/1018724/000119312517120198/d373368dex991.htm

51 'Microsoft CEO Satya Nadella: How Empathy Sparks Innovation', Knowledge@Wharton, 22 February 2018 http://knowledge.wharton.upenn.edu/article/microsofts-ceo-on-how-empathy-sparks-innovation/

52 Anthony, S (2014) *The First Mile – A Launch Manual for Getting Great Ideas into the Market,* Harvard Business Review Press, Boston, MA

53 'Talking Bullsh*t With Management Guru Tom Peters', Corporate Rebels, 21 January 2018 https://corporate-rebels.com/tom-peters/

54 Rana Foroohar, *Financial Times*, 29 January 2018 https://www.ft.com/content/18200d7c-02de-11e8-9650-9c0ad2d7c5b5

55 https://nzhistory.govt.nz/people/ernest-rutherford

56 Cable, D (2018) *Alive at Work – The Neuroscience of Helping Your People Love What They Do*, Harvard Business Review Press, Boston, MA

57 Barsh, J, Cranston, S and Craske, RA, 'Centered leadership: How talented women thrive', *McKinsey Quarterly,* September 2008 https://www.mckinsey.com/featured-insights/leadership/centered-leadership-how-talented-women-thrive

58 Fine, C (2017) *Testosterone Rex – Myths of Sex, Science and Society*, WW Norton & Co, New York, NY

59 'Women on Boards: 5 year summary' (Davies review), 29 October 2015 https://www.gov.uk/government/publications/women-on-boards-5-year-summary-davies-review

60 Reding, V, 'The Tug-of-War over the Women Quota,' 12 July 2012, Munich http://europa.eu/rapid/press-release_SPEECH-12-547_en.htm

61 'Turning the tables: ending sexual harassment at work', Equality and Human Rights Commission, 27 March 2018 https://www.equalityhumanrights.com/en/publication-download/turning-tables-ending-sexual-harassment-work

62 Wittenberg-Cox, A, 'How CEOs Can Put Gender Balance on the Agenda at Their Companies', *Harvard Business Review*, 30 November 2016 https://hbr.org/2016/11/how-ceos-can-put-gender-balance-on-the-agenda-at-their-companies

63 'Women, Parents and Career Progression: A Talk for Leaders Plus', House of Commons, March 2018 https://medium.com/@maja.korica/women-and-career-progression-a- talk-for-leaders-plus-house-of-commons-march-2018-2203893dfb7b

64 'The Purposeful Company', Big Innovation Centre, February 2017 http://www.biginnovationcentre.com/purposeful-company

65 'How to Avoid F**king Up on Purpose', Kin and Co, 25 January 2018 http://www.kinandco.com/its-official-businesses-are-fking-up-on-purpose/

66 Goffee, R, Jones, G and Steare, R, 'What would a moral organisation look like?', *Management Today,* 19 March 2018 https://www.managementtoday.co.uk/moral-organisation-look-like/any-other-business/article/1459771

67 https://www.blackrock.com/corporate/investor-relations/larry-fink-ceo-letter

68 'Purpose Powered Success', Korn Ferry Institute, 20 December 2016 https://www.kornferry.com/institute/purpose-powered-success

69 Goffee, R, Jones, G and Steare, R, 'What would a moral organisation look like?' *Management Today*, 19 March 2018 https://www.managementtoday.co.uk/moral-organisationlook-like/any-other-business/article/1459771

70 'How Can Investors Tell If a Company Is Genuinely Purpose-led?', A Blueprint for Better Business, https://www.blueprintforbusiness.org/

71 'A Purpose that Serves Society', A Blueprint for Better Business, http://www.blueprintforbusiness.org/purpose/

72 Coyle, D (2018) *The Culture Code – The Secret of Highly Successful Groups,* Random House Business, New York, NY

73 Stiglitz, JE, 'Post Davos Depression', Project Syndicate, 1 February 2018 https://www.project-syndicate.org/commentary/davos-ceos-tax-cuts-trump-by-joseph-e--stiglitz-2018-02

74 https://www.sharedvalue.org/partners/thought-leaders/
michael-e-porter

75 'Why is a Harvard Business Professor Studying Independent
Bookstores?', Literary Hub, 9 March 2018 https://lithub.
com/why-is-a-harvard-business-professor-studying-
independent-bookstores/

76 From the Boutwood Lecture: O'Neill, O, 'Justice without
Ethics: A 20th Century Innovation?' delivered 23 February
2017, Corpus Christi College, Cambridge

77 Campbell, A, 'Corporate Reputation: Alastair Campbell', *PR
Week,* 3 October 2012 https://www.prweek.com/
article/1152051/corporate-reputation-alastair-campbell-
portland---nine-lessons-strategy

78 Rumelt, R (2011) *Good Strategy, Bad Strategy: The Difference
and Why It Matters*, Crown Business, New York, NY

79 Martin, R and Lafley, AG (2013) *Playing to Win: How
Strategy Really Works*, Harvard Business Review Press,
Boston, MA

80 Mintzberg, H (1994) *The Rise and Fall of Strategic Planning*,
Free Press, New York, NY

81 Mintzberg, H, Lampel, J and Ahlstrand, B (2004) *Strategy
Bites Back*, FT Prentice Hall, London

82 Gerstner Jr, Louis V, (2002) *Who Says Elephants Can't
Dance?* HarperCollins, New York NY

83 Sull, D, 'Look Out for the Tunnel Vision Trap', *Financial
Times,* August 2004 https://www.ft.com/content/e0bcb1ac-
e576-11d8-bfd2-00000e2511c8

84 Umoh, R, 'Billionaire Jeff Bezos says being smart isn't
enough – you also need this to be successful', CNBC, 21
September 2017 https://www.cnbc.com/2017/09/21/
why-billionaire-jeff-bezos-says-being-smart-isnt-enough-to-
succeed.html

85 Marble, D, 'Jeff Bezos Quit His Job at 30 to Launch
    Amazon – Here Are the 3 Simple Strategies He Used to Do It',
    Inc., https://www.inc.com/darren-marble/jeff-bezos-quit-his-
    job-at-30-to-launch-amazon-heres-how-to-know-if-its-right-
    time-for-your-big-move.html

86 Clifford, C, 'How Amazon founder Jeff Bezos went from the
    son of a teen mom to the world's richest person', CNBC, 27
    Oct 2017 https://www.cnbc.com/2017/10/27/how-amazon-
    founder-jeff-bezos-went-from-the-son-of-a-teen-mom-to-the-
    worlds-richest-person.html

87 Kantor, J, Streitfield, D, 'Inside Amazon: Wrestling Big Ideas in
    a Bruising Workplace', *New York Times*, 16 August 2015
    https://www.nytimes.com/2015/08/16/technology/inside-
    amazon-wrestling-big-ideas-in-a-bruising-workplace.html

88 https://finance.yahoo.com/news/mark-cuban-says-follows-
    advice-185854492.html?guccounter=1

89 Jeff Bezos, Amazon Shareholder Letter, April 2017 https://
    www.cnbc.com/2017/04/12/amazon-jeff-bezos-2017-
    shareholder-letter.html

90 https://hcz.org/about-us/leadership/geoffrey-canada/

91 Harris, P, 'Can Geoffrey Canada rescue America's ailing
    schools? Barack Obama hopes so', *Guardian,* 10 October
    2010 https://www.theguardian.com/world/2010/oct/10/
    harlem-schools-learning-revolution

92 Canada, G, 'Our failing schools. Enough is enough!' TED
    Talk, May 2013 https://www.ted.com/talks/geoffrey_
    canada_our_failing_schools_enough_is_enough

93 Ignatius, A, 'Businesses Exist to Deliver Value to Society',
    Harvard Business Review, March– April 2018 https://hbr.
    org/2018/03/businesses-exist-to-deliver-value-to-society

94 Erman, M, 'Three CEOs resign from Trump Council Over
    Charlottesville', Reuters, 14 August 2017 https://uk.reuters.

    com/article/us-virginia-protests-merck/three-ceos-resign-from-trump-council-over-charlottesville-idUKKCN1AU1FM

95 Drucker, P (1946) *Concept of the Corporation*, John Day Company, New York, NY

96 https://www.linkedin.com/pulse/first-90-days-new-job-mary-barra/

97 Kane, L, 'When Pepsi CEO Indra Nooyi got her pivotal promotion, her mother cut off the announcement and sent her out to get milk instead', UK Business Insider, 2 August 2017, http://uk.businessinsider.com/pepsi-indra-nooyi-work-life-balance-2017-8

98 Stern, S, 'Outsider in a hurry to shake up Unilever', *Financial Times*, April 2010, https://www.ft.com/content/fa865f42-3ff3-11df-8d23-00144feabdc0

99 'Can Unilever's Paul Polman change the way we do business?' https://www.ft.com/content/e6696b4a-8505-11e6-8897-2359a58ac7a5

100 https://www.npr.org/templates/story/story.php?storyId=4973548&t=1538496381128

101 'What is leadership?' Britain Thinks, July 2012 http://britainthinks.com/pdfs/What-is-Leadership-2.pdf

102 Mattinson, D, 'Today's political leaders are all in Winston Churchill's shadow, say voters', *Guardian*, 6 December 2015 https://www.theguardian.com/politics/2015/dec/06/britainthinks-political-leaders-shadow-winston-churchill

103 'What does Britain want from its leaders?' Britain Thinks, 5 September 2017, http://britainthinks.com/pdfs/BritainThinks-Leadership-Study-2017.pdf

104 Churchill, W, 'War Office Memorandum', 12 May 1919 https://www.nationalchurchillmuseum.org/churchills-1919-war-office-memorandum.html

105　Mukerjee, M (2010) *Churchill's Secret War – The British Empire and the Ravaging of India During World War Two*, Basic Books, New York, NY

106　Ingersoll, R, *Report on England,* Simon and Schuster, New York, 1940

107　Wearmounth, R, 'Actor Michael Sheen Heightens Speculation He Could Stand To Be A Labour MP', Huffington Post, 25 March 2018 https://www.huffingtonpost.co.uk/entry/michael-sheen-labour-mp_uk_5ab771aee4b0decad04ad210

108　'From Leonardo da Vinci to Steve Jobs: The Benefits of Being a Misfit', Knowledge@Wharton, 17 January 2018 http://knowledge.wharton.upenn.edu/article/leonardo-da-vinci-steve-jobs-benefits-misfit/?utm_source=kw_newsletter&utm_medium=email&utm_campaign=2018-01-18

109　Ibid.

110　Taylor, B, 'Why the Future Belongs to Tough-Minded Optimists', *Harvard Business Review,* 3 March 2016 https://hbr.org/2016/03/why-the-future-belongs-to-tough-minded-optimists

111　http://knowledge.wharton.upenn.edu/article/leonardo-da-vinci-steve-jobs-benefits-misfit/?utm_source=kw_newsletter&utm_medium=email&utm_campaign=2018-01-18

112　Ibarra, H (2015) *Act Like a Leader, Think Like a Leader*, Harvard Business Review Press, Boston, MA

INDEX

Heffernan, Margaret 2
Hemingway, Ernest 39; *The Sun Also Rises* 38
Hilsenrath, Rebecca 78–9
hope, inspiring and providing 45–6
hype, belief in your own 40–1

Ibarra, Professor Herminia: *Act Like a Leader, Think Like a Leader* 134
IBM 98
Immelt, Jeff 13
important leaders, a few 102–26 *see also individual leader name*
indecision 33–7
Ingersoll, Ralph 125–6
innovation: disruptive 26–7; humility and 68; start-ups and 55
Isaacson, Walter 51, 128, 131, 133

Jericho Partners 2
Jobs, Steve 4, 128, 131, 133, 134
Johnson, Dr 17
Jones, Gareth 15, 17–18, 86, 87, 134

kaizen (continuous improvement) 26
Kay, John 89, 93, 97
Kelleher, Herb 19, 21, 94
Kelly, Walt 85
Kennedy, John F. 1, 16
Kerry, John 33
Keytruda 109
Kin&Co 85–6
King, Dr Martin Luther: *Stride Toward Freedom* 122
knowledge economy 8
Kodak 41
Korica, Dr Maja 83–4
Korn Ferry Institute 87
Kotter, Professor John: *A Sense of Urgency* 29, 132
Kraft 116, 118
Kramer, Mark 91

Lafley, AG 42–3, 96; *Playing to Win: How Strategy Really Works* 96–7, 99

language, leader 1, 85–101; purpose 85–9; strategy 93–8; values 89–93; vision 98–101
leadership: bad leaders 22–37; belief and 127–9; business type and 54–69; crisis in 1–5; goal setting and 129–31; good leaders 38–53; important leaders 102–26; language of 85–101; meaning of 7–21; persistence and 131–4; size of industry 1; women/gender balance and 70–84
Leahy, Sir Terry 13, 52
learned skill, leadership as a 37
learning, appetite for 49–53
Lehman Brothers 73
listening: active 12, 48, 59; to women 77
LitHub 91
London Business School 68
Lyft 114

Maccoby, Michael: 'Narcissistic leaders: the incredible pros, the inevitable cons' 23–6, 45
Management Today 86
March, James 10
Marks and Spencer 40
Martin, Roger: *Playing to Win: How Strategy Really Works* 96–7, 99
Mattinson, Deborah 123
Maven 114
maximum optionality 36
Mayer, Colin 119–20
McCauley, Clark 87
McGill University 97
McKinsey 23, 58, 71, 72, 97
McKinsey Quarterly 71–2
mentors 72, 76
Mercer, Johnny 2
Merck 108–12
Michelangelo 48
Microsoft 49, 53, 99
Minchin, Tim 3
Mintzberg, Henry: *The Rise and Fall of Strategic Planning* 97; *Strategy Bites Back* (with Joe Lampel and Bruce Ahlstrand) 97